OAST  IN SUSSEX AND KENT

Their History and Development

Frontispiece. The Oasthouse at Hastings Priory Farm from a lithograph entitled 'Remains of Hastings Priory' drawn and published by J. Rouse, 1823. The building must have stood somewhere near the present site of Sainsbury's in the centre of Hastings. The two vents to the inset kiln suggest a mid-to-late eighteenth-century date - a period when other such conversions are known to have been made. This picture and another sketch by Rouse are the only remaining evidence of the appearance of this building.
(The photograph of the lithograph, taken by Peter Greenhalf A.R.P.S., is reproduced here by kind permission of Hastings Museum & Art Gallery.)

OASTHOUSES
IN SUSSEX AND KENT

Their History and Development

By

Gwen Jones
and
John Bell

Published by

PHILLIMORE

for

HOP INDUSTRY RESEARCH SURVEY
1992

Published by
PHILLIMORE & CO. LTD.
Shopwyke Hall,
Chichester, Sussex, England

for
HOP INDUSTRY RESEARCH SURVEY

ISBN   0 85033 818 2

Cover Illustration: An Oasthouse near Tenterden, Kent. This is one of the few traditional oasthouses in south-east England which is still used for drying hops. Not all the kilns remain in use, however. The roundel on the left is redundant and only the two square kilns are used. (*The photograph is reproduced here by kind permission of Mr. G.H. Delemare.*)

CONTENTS

The Hop Industry Research Survey was set up in 1981 in response to the increase in the rate of conversion or demolition of oasthouses. It exists in order to record those buildings which remain and which materially add to our knowledge of the industry. All ought, at least, to be inspected and some should be recorded in detail. If any reader knows of one which has escaped inspection or seems particularly interesting, would they please contact Mrs. Gwen Jones at 9, Cockcrow Wood, St. Leonards, East Sussex   TN37 7HW.

FOREWORD

.... 'I need only notice the oast houses in use in the county of Kent. Are there any two of these alike ? Is not some arrangement in each different from that adopted in others ? Has not every farmer some favourite plan of his own ? To describe even a portion of these would be an endless task. . . .'

Viscount Torrington 1845. [1]

Lord Torrington was right. Each oasthouse is different from all the others in some way, not just in Kent but wherever they were built. The sheer numbers of them built is testimony to the importance of hops in the agrarian history of the south and east of England and it was the realisation of their seemingly infinite variety which led us to undertake their recording. In seeking to understand the differences observable in each building and in trying to assign a date to the alterations which were visible in most of them, we came to formulate the broad outline of their development.

From that point we could turn to the many surviving documents which speak of hop growing in former centuries. Their details, however, are frequently much narrower in scope and only a few throw light on the industry as a whole. The buildings themselves really are crucial to a proper understanding of the history of the industry.

Given the recent acceleration in the decline of the Hop Industry and in the conversion or demolition of its buildings, we undertook Lord Torrington's "endless task" because, in conversion, oasthouses usually lose most of their significant details. Our record is not just a 'description' but consists of scaled drawings and photographs with recourse to historical documents wherever possible. The following account of the way oasthouses developed is therefore based on the architectural and historical evidence of the buildings themselves.

The book could not have been written without the kindness and interest of the many owners who have given us permission to record, and sometimes to excavate their property. Our work has been voluntary and has been funded almost entirely by talks and lectures given on the work completed. We therefore owe a special debt of gratitude to the following owners who made generous donations towards the cost of publication: Mr. and Mrs. A. Faulkner, Mr. and Mrs. P. Gunnery, Mr. and Mrs. N. Walker. We wish to thank the following people for help with illustrations: Mr. G.H. Delemare for the Cover Illustration; Hastings Museum & Art Gallery and Mr. P. Greenhalf for the frontispiece; Mr. and Mrs. D. Martin for Fig. 10; Mr. P.H. Dunn for Fig. 12; Mr. P. Gillies for Fig. 40; *Hastings & St. Leonards Observer* for Fig. 42; Mr. A. Dickinson for Fig. 44A; Mr. W. John Smith and Mr. J. Duly for making black and white copies of some of our slides. We acknowledge with special gratitude the help so generously given by Mr. Kenneth Gravett in setting up the publication of this booklet. We would also like to thank all members of the staffs of the East Sussex Record Office and the Kent Archives Office for their help and guidance.

Gwen Jones   *John Bell*

vii

Fig. 1   The Scale of the Industry:

Fig. 1A   Golford's Oast, Cranbrook, Kent. This building is thought to date from the 1740s but in size and plan differed little from oasthouses of the late sixteenth century. It served a very small acreage of probably no more than 1-2 acres.

Fig. 1B   Whitbread's Hop Farm, Beltring, Kent. The core of this complex dates from the late nineteenth century and it grew to this size in the twentieth century, under the management of the brewery. Up to 200 acres of hops were dried here.

INTRODUCTION
Background to the Industry

Beer is traditionally the drink of the Englishman but this tradition takes no real account of the revolution in beer brewing which took place, in England at least, over the fourteenth and fifteenth centuries. It was then that hopped beer as opposed to unhopped ale (until then the 'traditional' brew), became accepted.

Beer brewing had increased on the continent from the thirteenth century onwards and it is clear that it was even then appreciated in England: in 1289 a Norwich ale-seller imported some for sale and was subsequently charged with 'selling Flanders beer privily'. More widespread introduction aroused quite a lot of initial hostility, but gradually beer increased in popularity. In 1400 it was being imported into Winchelsea and within a few years hops themselves were being imported for brewing beer in this country. Flemings and Dutchmen were the first to brew hopped beer here. When in 1436 attacks were made on foreign beer brewers in London, this resulted in the passing of an Act of Parliament by Henry VI which allowed them to remain and to continue their trade. By the end of the fifteenth century most of the prejudices against the use of this 'additive' had been overcome and beer was brewed by native brewers in almost every town in the kingdom.[2]

Hops are grown from cuttings or 'sets'* which in the past could be bought locally from many of the large growers. They take two to three years to mature and the plants then will continue to produce their cones for a further ten to fifteen years when planted in poorer soils, and for up to fifty years in better soils. Hops produce a perfumed yellow resin* or pollen, which both imparts the bitter flavour to the beer and also acts as a preservative. The beer can then be kept in good condition for much longer than had been possible with unhopped ale, and the preservative quality gives the advantage of allowing the beer to be transported, exported even - as the Flemings had proved - without immediate deterioration.

Hops are a labour intensive crop in every stage of their production. First they need to be planted 1.8m. to 2.1m. (6 to 7 ft.) apart in a specially prepared ground usually called a hop garden or a hop yard. Poles, replaced more recently by a complicated system of wires and strings, are needed for their growth and they demand rich manuring and constant attention to cultivation as well as a series of measures to counteract the pests and diseases to which they are all too prone.

The labour does not end once the hops are picked: to be of most value to the brewer they need to be dried and it was for this process that oasthouses were developed (Fig. 1). After the drying it became standard practice to tread them into pockets* or bags* in order to exclude the air and to preserve as large a quantity as possible of the resin.

---

* An asterisk denotes that the term is included in the Glossary, page 69.

1

In England, notably in Kent, Sussex, Surrey, Herefordshire, Worcestershire and Hampshire, up to four centuries of experience went towards the perfecting of the process of drying and pressing as practised by the growers until recently. Although grown in other counties as well, hops there had largely disappeared from the farms by the end of the nineteenth century. That century saw both the peak years of the industry and the beginning of its decline and to those peak years most of the oasthouses now familiar in the landscape belong; by the mid-nineteenth century an oasthouse had to be provided for any grower who seriously hoped to make a good profit from his hops.

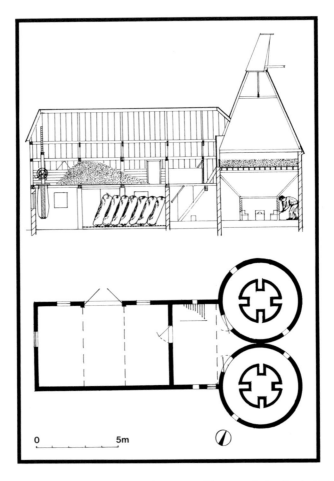

Fig. 2   Diagram of the Function of the Oasthouse. Hops are drying in the Kiln and the fires below are being tended. Other hops dried previously have cooled on the floor and the press is ready to receive them. An empty pocket has been suspended into the sling, which will support it when the press is in action. The pockets already filled are being stored on the ground floor.

2

CHAPTER 1
The Function of the Oasthouse

Farmers have probably known the principles of drying from prehistoric times; corn-drying kilns have certainly been in use since Roman times and malt kilns are known from mediaeval days. The simple principle of convection was applied: all that was necessary was a source of heat on or in the ground, some form of perforated floor above, on which was spread the substance to be dried, and sufficient expertise to know when the right level of desiccation had been achieved. The first experiments in drying hops must have been on such kilns; the expertise grew with the industry.

Essentially the familiar oasthouse had five main functions:
(1) to receive the green hops after they had been picked off the bine;
(2) to dry them in the kiln;
(3) to provide space for their controlled cooling after removal from the kiln;
(4) to provide facilities for pressing them into long bags called 'pockets'; and
(5) to provide storage space for the pockets until they were sent to market.

In order to fulfil those functions the buildings were divided into two areas:
a) the kiln or kilns, where the hops would be dried; and
b) the stowage, where the hops would first be received, then after drying, cooled, pressed or bagged, and stored.

By the nineteenth century there were usually two floors to both stowage and kilns (Fig. 2).

The Kilns

The Ground Floor

The kilns of the oasthouses familiar today are either square or round and built either at one end of the stowage or alongside it, with intercommunicating doors between stowage and kiln on both floors.

The ground floor housed the source of heat and this could be provided by an enclosed grate, by a honeycombed brick furnace or by fires lit in open grates. Where an enclosed stove was used, a system of pipes carried the heat up to concentrate it close to the drying floor (see Fig. 20). The honeycombed brick furnace stood in the centre or just inside the door of the kiln, and above it often hung a spark plate* which also helped to spread the heat across the full width of the drying floor. Open grates were normally screened by a wall which either funnelled outwards to join the external wall of the kiln just below the drying floor or formed a tunnel across the centre (Fig.3).

Using charcoal and anthracite as fuel, drying could take anything up to fourteen to sixteen hours. Once the fires were lit, the heat was gradually intensified to about 60°C (140°F) to drive off the moisture before being allowed to fall to about 49°C (120°F) again.[3] It was crucial to keep the fires lit and the temperature controlled throughout the process. Undue loss of heat meant damage to that load of hops. If the fires actually went out the load was totally spoiled.

Where any form of open firing was used it was important to have a good intake of air at the right level in order to keep the fires constant. Small openings were constructed in the lowest courses of the walls of the kilns and these openings had, usually on the inside face of the wall, wooden shutters which could be raised or lowered according to the need to increase or lessen the draught.

Where an enclosed stove or furnace was in use, draught was sometimes ducted under the floor. In these kilns a small window was often built into the external wall so that the drier could see what he was doing. With brickwork furnaces or open fires the drier normally relied upon the firelight to see by.

The First Floor

In order to allow the heat from the fires to pass through the hops the joists of the first floor supported slats of either timber or metal, although in some kilns perforated tiles were used instead. Where a tiled floor was used, there was no danger of the hops falling through onto the fires because the perforations were too small; where the drying floor was slatted, a coarsely woven cloth of horsehair was laid over the slats and either looped over hooks in the kiln wall or tacked to a timber plate recessed into the wall just above the floor. This cloth then kept the hops from falling down between the slats and reduced waste and the danger of fire.

Onto this 'hair', as it was called, the pokes* of green hops were emptied, usually to a depth of 400mm. (16 in.) or so. The load of hops emptied into the kiln would vary according to whether the season was wet or dry and, therefore, to the levels of moisture in the hops themselves. When the hops were loaded, they were levelled with a widely toothed rake to ensure even drying. The length of the drying depended upon the depth of the load. A good draught was essential to pull the hot air up through the hops and then out at the top of the kiln. Cowls which swung round against the wind and created a vacuum helped pull up the hot air, thereby increasing the speed at which the hops would dry. They are believed to have been introduced during the middle years of the eighteenth century.[4]

The Stowage

The Ground Floor

The layout of the ground floor of the stowage was dictated by the position of the kilns. Adjacent to them there was usually a partitioned area which might serve all or any of three main purposes:
(1) to screen the area in order to allow a controlled intake of air into the kilns whose doors normally incorporated some form of shuttered opening;
(2) to allow the driers some comfort: they normally did not leave the building while the drying was in process (beds or armchairs were often brought in);
(3) to house a convenient supply of fuel.

4

The rest of the ground floor might then be used to store the pockets until they were despatched and in some oasthouses special raised and slatted racks were installed in order to allow free passage of air around them. They were normally stored upside down so that, in years when they were stored for a long period, the damage possible to the hops at the bottom from the sheer weight of the contents could easily be remedied by re-opening the sewn end and replacing the damaged hops.

The First Floor

In traditional oasthouses green hops arriving from the garden were received directly into the first floor of the building. The loosely woven pokes, used to transport them, prevented them from sweating and growing hot, which caused deterioration. Care was taken to get each load of hops into the kiln as quickly as possible after picking. Once large acreages were grown and large amounts of hops were arriving at the oasthouses for drying, 'greenstages'* with widely slatted floors were introduced, again to prevent sweating (cf. Fig. 31).

When dry, the hops were removed from the kiln, heaped or spread over the floor of the stowage and left to cool. In most buildings familiar today the cooling area equalled or was just slightly greater than the area of the kilns. Its floor was closely boarded and its walls either fully or partially matchboarded (see, for example, Fig. 19). Where the walls were left unboarded, they were whitewashed. These were measures of 'hop hygiene' and served to prevent hop residues from collecting in the cracks and crannies, thereby becoming a source of contamination during the pressing.

When first removed from the kiln, the hops were extremely dry and brittle and if pressed in that condition would break or shatter. During the cooling process they re-absorbed some moisture from the air and became less fragile. Cooling times varied enormously and depended partly on the size of the load, partly on the temperature and humidity levels prevailing, and partly on the beliefs and practices of the drier himself. The hops might be left to lie for up to a day or more and recourse might be made to scientific instruments to measure temperature and humidity. More frequently, however, when the practised hand of the drier could take a hop, crush it and detect just the right amount of resistance in the leaves of the cone and when his equally experienced nose could perceive just the right pungency from the pollen, the hops were ready for pressing.

The first floor of the stowage had a trap opening into which a circular frame could be fitted and from this the pocket was suspended. Up to about 1850 a man got down into the pocket, the hops were shovelled in and he carefully trod them down beneath him until the hops, tightly compressed, filled the whole pocket. About 1850 a mechanical press was patented and widely adopted on the farms: it took ten to fifteen minutes to fill the pocket whereas a man's feet had taken sixty ! (Fig. 4).

Once full, the pocket was sewn up, stencilled with the number of the pocket, the name of the farmer and the name and county of the farm, and was then stored on the ground floor until the samples were taken. This was a process normally carried out by an itinerant hop sampler who skilfully opened the side of the pocket and withdrew a block of hops which were then trimmed

5

Fig. 3   Four Examples of Firing:

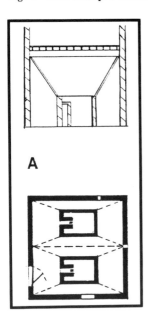

Fig. 3A The two fire-grates here were enclosed by brick walls to prevent loss of heat. Above the brickwork, walls of timber, lath and plaster extended to the outside walls, forming a hopper shape, which kept the heat contained, while allowing it to spread across the drying floor. Two such grates were sufficient here, whereas with open grates more would probably have been needed.

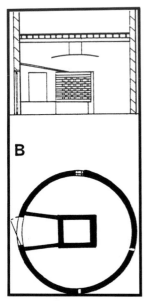

Fig. 3B This furnace consisted of a large honeycombed brick structure, with one large fire-grate at the centre and roofed over at the top. This roof helped to prevent sparks from reaching the drying floor and in many kilns a baffle plate was suspended over the furnace, both to prevent sparks from flying and to encourage the heat to spread right across the kiln. The covered passage prevented loss of heat from the kiln, but when the fire was really hot there was no protection for the drier. The area round the furnace was cleared of ash and debris via the door in the passage wall.

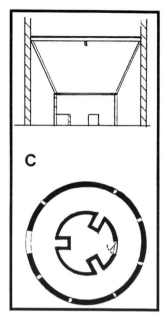

Fig. 3C The three grates were set behind a circular screening wall above which a wall of timber, lath and plaster extended to the outside wall of the kiln to form a firing tunnel, which protected the drier from the heat while allowing him easy access to all the grates. The hopper shape again contained the heat, while allowing it to spread across the drying floor. A door in the screening wall allowed the area behind the grates to be cleared.

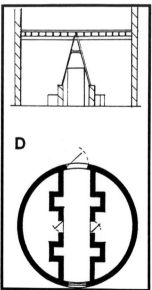

Fig. 3D Four open grates were set two either side of a central firing tunnel. Its walls both screened the drier and allowed him sight of all the grates. The heat was again contained behind walls of timber, lath and plaster, which joined to form a ridge, in order to allow the heat to spread across the kiln.

Fig. 4 A Treading Hole, typically sited in a corner. The pocket was nailed or suspended from a hoop and a man got down into the pocket and trod the hops in with his feet.

Fig. 5 The Cooling Floor and Press in use in a Modern Oasthouse. The hops have cooled and are being scuppeted towards the press, now power-driven, on the left.

8

into a neat rectangular packet. These were sent to the Hop Market and when the samples had been judged and bargained for, a process organised by the hop factors, the pockets from which the samples had been taken were sent up to market and sold.

As the following chapters will show, the oasthouse described did not take shape until the nineteenth century. With the innovations brought by the twentieth century it remained in general use until the 1960s and 1970s. Over the centuries, better heating and handling of hops improved their quality but that quality could never be guaranteed; there were too many variables whose control was beyond the power of the growers. The weather was obviously one. Very wet or very dry seasons greatly affected how and when the hop bines matured and produced their cones. Extremes of weather, wet or dry, also affected the incidence of hop diseases and insect attack. Heavy rainfall during September could lengthen the drying process and reduce the amount of hops which could be dried at any one time; it also adversely affected the condition of those still left unpicked.

The oasthouse was in itself another variable. Careful construction and design played their part in the fine control of the heat and in the efficient handling of the hops into and out of the kiln. This control and efficiency were also affected by the position of the oasthouse within the farmstead. Given that undue loss of heat at a crucial stage could severely reduce the money made from the dried crop, the oasthouse needed to be carefully sited to take advantage of even the gentlest breeze from any of the four quarters.

Then the knowledge and ability of the driers themselves varied. In many cases the skills of the craft were handed down from father to son and their expertise was recognised in the rates of pay which oast work could command. Just occasionally, adherence to traditional methods led to obstinate prejudice in the face of new ideas. Once accepted, however, successive innovations and experiments brought hop drying to the pitch of perfection attainable today when controlled cultivation and the use of highly sophisticated machinery can almost guarantee a dried crop of uniform quality. Such techniques and installations depend on capital; its availability or the lack of it remains the most crucial variable of all.

Whenever possible, a suitably draughty position next to the farm pond was adopted for oasthouses because of the ever-present danger of fire - quite a number did burn down. Where possible, it was also better to have them conveniently close to a road in order to get the hops to market. When the last bags or pockets had finally gone, and that was sometimes not until April of the following year, the building would remain in use for storing implements and husbandry tackle on the ground floor, for grain or seeds on the first floor. On small farms some even served as stables or cattle sheds.

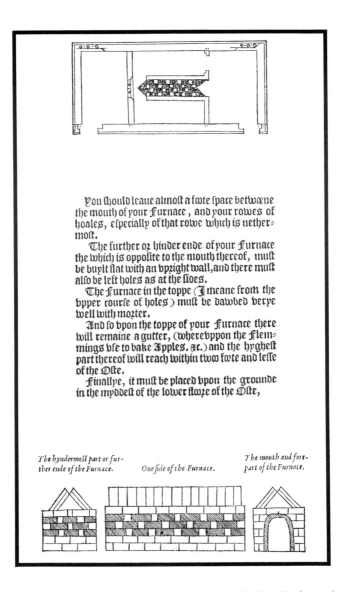

You ſhould leaue almoſt a fœte ſpace betwœne the mouth of pour Furnace, and pour rowes of hoales, eſpecially of that rowe whict is nether= moſt.

The further oʒ hinder ende of pour Furnace the which is oppoſite to the mouth thereof, muſt be buplt flat with an bpʒight wall, and there muſt alſo be left holes as at the ſides.

The Furnace in the toppe (J meane from the bpper courſe of holes) muſt be dawbed berpe well with moʒter.

And ſo bpon the toppe of pour Furnace there will remaine a gutter, (wherebpon the Flem= mings bſe to bake Apples. ꝛc.) and the hpgheſt part thereof will reach within twœ fœte and leſſe of the Oſte.

Finallpe, it muſt be placed bpon the grounde in the mpddeſt of the lower ſtwʒe of the Oſte,

The hyndermoſt part or fur-ther ende of the Furnace.   *One ſide of the Furnace.*   *The mouth and fore-part of the Furnace.*

Fig. 6 Two Sixteenth-century Illustrations taken from *A Perfite Platform of a Hoppe Garden* by Reynolde Scot. The Plan shows a small timber-framed building partitioned into three units. At one end the green hops were received and then loaded into the square kiln in the middle. At the other end the dried hops were removed from the kiln via the hatch and then bagged on the ground floor or trodden into a long bag suspended from a treading hole. The kiln was heated by a wood fire set within the honeycombed brick furnace illustrated. This furnace, shown in the second edition of 1576, already marks a technological advance in that the brick structure, although shorter, is considerably taller and presumably more efficient.

CHAPTER 2
Early Oasthouses in England

The adoption of beer brewing resulted in rising levels of imports of hops during the sixteenth century. The records for Robertsbridge Abbey Furnace show that hops, perhaps imported ones, were being bought in 1542 for the beer brewed for the workers, some of whom were themselves from the Low Countries.[5] A Rye brewery had a 'hoppehouse' by 1585 and hops are listed amongst the imports which came through the port in the 1580s.[6] The numbers of foreigners arriving on ships no doubt ensured that hopped beer was in demand.

Things were changing, however. We know that Sussex farmers were beginning to look upon hops as a profitable crop, because in 1589 the Mayfield parish register recorded the death of one of the itinerant specialists who travelled the countryside setting up hop gardens.[7]

Some farmers, at least, must have kiln-dried the hops they grew but very few, if any, of the oasthouses they built remain standing, and our only knowledge of them comes from a tract published in 1574 by Reynolde Scot, called 'A Perfite Platform of a Hoppe Garden'.[8] (Fig. 6). His idea in writing the book was precisely to encourage English farmers to take up hop growing in order to make for themselves the profit that the Flemings were clearly receiving from their exports. He explained how to set up the garden and the main points of cultivation as practised in Belgium, then turned his attention to the oasthouse: 'to show you by description such an Oste as they drie their Hoppes upon at Poppering, with the order thereof etc. which for the small charges and trouble in drying, for the speedie and well drying, and for the handsome and easie dooing thereof, maybe a profytable patterne.'

His stress on good drying practices is important, even though he optimistically made it all sound much simpler and much less expensive than it probably turned out to be. Elsewhere in the text he had made it clear that drying on what he called a 'common oste' (a malt or corn drying kiln), was not good enough, and that only a purpose-built oasthouse would do.

The small size of the building, approximately 5.79m. (19 ft.) long by 2.44m. (8 ft.) wide, was appropriate for the size of crop the farmers were likely to be growing: 0.20 to 0.40 hectares (half to one acre) - very rarely more. His specifications were for a timber-framed building, although he said that brick would be better because there would be less risk of fire. Inside were three separate rooms of which the biggest was the kiln. It was placed in the middle and on the ground floor was walled off into a 'close, square room,' - 5.95m². (64 sq.ft.) - with a furnace built of honeycombed brickwork in the centre. The slatted drying floor was set 1.52m. (5 ft.) above the ground and at first floor level the walls round this were built up to a height of 1.22m. (4 ft.), to prevent the load of hops from spreading (Fig. 6).

The two rooms, each 1.52m. by 2.44m. (5 ft. by 8 ft.), were to be for the green hops on one side of the kiln and for the dried hops on the other. There is initially no indication that these two rooms were floored at first floor level and

11

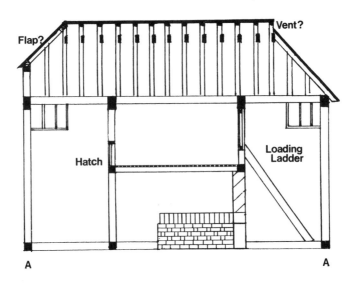

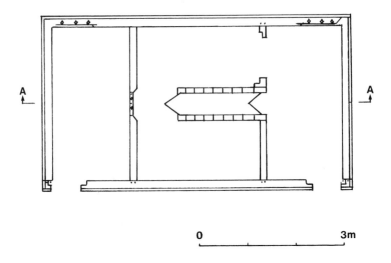

0 ⊢————————————————⊣ 3m

Fig. 7 **A Reconstruction** based on the details given by Reynolde Scot. Its small size and utilitarian simplicity are the principal features. The furnace is the forerunner of the larger one used later (Fig. 3B). The hatch for emptying the kiln and the lack of roof ventilation are typical of the period.

12

they may well have been left unfloored, or only partially floored to provide a loading and unloading platform either side of the kiln. A small hatch was provided just above the drying floor 'to throwe off from the bed the dryed hoppes, downe into the roume belowe prepared for them'. The fire was to be made in a brick-built furnace 325mm. (13 in.) wide, 1.5m. to 2.1m. (5 ft. to 7 ft.) long but only 325mm. (13 in.) high ! Yet it had to have 'hoales at each side, the length of one Bricke asunder, and the bygness of halfe a Bricke, placed checkerwise' (1574).

This surely must have been an error and the reprint of 1576 gives instructions for a furnace approximately 609mm. (2 ft.) high but shorter, only 762mm. (2 ft. 6 in.) long. In view of the changes in dimension in the different editions, it would seem that Scot himself was uncertain of the exact details. There is at least more chance of successfully following his instructions in 1576: 'Before you beginne to make your hoales, you should laye two rowes of Bricke, and when your three ranks of hoales are placed upon them you must laye again over them one other rowe of Brycke, and uppon the same you must place your last and highest course, and they must stand longwyse (as it were a tiptoe) the toppes of the Brickes meeting together above (the nether part of them resting upon the uppermost course) and note that till then eche side must be built alongst directly upwarde' (1576).

The drying floor was to be made of rails or slats 'sawen verye even, one ynche square and layde one quarter of an ynche asunder'. The hops were to be loaded 457mm. (18 in.) deep with the slats set so closely that no hair cloth was needed, a point on which Scot was curiously insistent 'and note that upon this Oste, there is no Oste cloth to be used' - perhaps feeling that the cloth would act as an impediment to speedy drying. This seems to underlie his thought when he goes on to say that for 'a common oste' a cloth would be necessary to prevent the hops from falling down onto the fire below and that the hops in these were to be laid no more than 220 to 225mm. (8 or 9 in.) deep, 'yet would still take longer to dry'. The roof is unfortunately not detailed and we are left to assume that either the hot air passed out through a window or that some sort of opening was made in the roof structure.

Surprisingly, wood is recommended for the fuel. Old and broken poles were to be used when kindling it but 'for the continuance and maintenance of this fyre that woode is best which is not too drie'. It is not surprising that he warns against burning dry hop bines or straw, both of which would flare, nor that he advises against too much stirring of the fire although it was to be kept continual and hot.

He is careful to include instructions for the treading of the hops after drying. The art was clearly in its infancy. The sack was to be doubled over to guard against tearing and then pinned to two cross beams using four 152mm. (6 in.) pins. (See Fig. 19, for a late example of a pressing platform.) A rope was to be passed underneath the sack and tied to the beams. A man could then get into the sack to tread the hops with his feet. The operation was obviously felt to be possible because 'before the sacke be halfe full, it will rest upon the grounde, whereby you shall be able to presse them harder together'. Nevertheless, the hazards, not to say deficiencies of the task were apparent: 'the handsommer waye were to make a square hole (as wyde as the sackes mouth) in the floore of the Lofte . . . . and to hang downe your sacke at that hoale . . . .' (See Fig. 4 for an early example of this).

13

Despite one or two omissions, from Scot's description emerges an archetypal image of the purpose-built oasthouses of the time. Recognising that some farmers had already adopted hops as a crop, he makes allowances for larger acreages by recommending a slightly larger building:

'If your Garden be verye great, you may buylde your house somewhat larger, namely XXII foot longe and 10ft. broade and then you must make in this Oste two furnaces two or three foote asunder, placing the doore betwixt them both, otherwise in all pointes like to that which I first described'.

Both buildings were small in comparison with later ones but it will be noted that the process described in the nineteenth-century oast above - reception, drying, cooling and pressing - had changed in little but the measure of sophistication brought to it. If the loading and unloading of the kiln and its venting seem rather primitive in Scot's oasthouse, as does the pressing operation first described, nevertheless important points were clearly well understood. The building was constructed with care taken to exclude unwanted draught, and brick was used for the walls adjacent to the furnace to lessen the fire risk. In one important aspect, however, Scot's building was superior to most of those of succeeding centuries in 'throughput': the hops went in at one end and came out duly processed at the other. This was a point of efficiency which appears to have been lost in many oasthouses during the seventeenth century and not regained in all, until the twentieth.

Fig. 8   A Malthouse of 1652, Buxted Parish, East Sussex. The original elevation has been altered: the large doors have been inserted and the infilling in the brickwork reveals the former presence of a ground-floor window and a first-floor door.

14

CHAPTER 3
Seventeenth-Century Developments

The reason why few early oasthouses have survived must be that they quickly became too small. A clear picture of mid-seventeenth-century acreages is given in the Tithe Book of John Lord, the vicar of Salehurst, East Sussex.[9] In this he recorded the tithe rents* due to him from his parishioners, most of whom appear to have been fairly constantly in arrears! Because extra rent was demanded for hops they were usually noted separately, which makes it easy to see what acreages were being grown.

All the hops are recorded in 'hop acres', but these were not a constant measurement: the acres were determined by counting the numbers of hills. One thousand hills* made one hop acre. They covered an area which was normally smaller than the statute acre. (In the nineteenth century a statute acre usually contained 1200 hills.) Table 1 below shows how small most of the hop gardens were at that time.

TABLE 1
Acreages of Hops 1647-1659

Hop acres	No. of hop gardens
0 - 1	18
1 - 2	33
2 - 3	6
3 - 4	1
4 - 5	1
5 - 6	0
6 - 7	1

Source: John Lord's *Tithe Book*. E.S.R.O. PAR 377/6/1/1

The norm for sixteenth-century hop gardens is believed to have been half to one 'hop acre'. Table 1 shows a clear advance on that estimate even though the gardens remained small by modern standards: by the mid-seventeenth century 70% of the hop gardens were larger than one 'hop acre'. Not every one belonged to different farmers, however: while there were 60 separate plantations, only 47 farmers were named, so it is clear that several of them owned or tenanted more than one garden, often on different farms. When the figures have been adjusted to take these farmers into account there is a total of only 12 (26%) who were growing less than one hop acre; 25 (53%) growing between 1 and 2 hop acres; 6 (13%) growing between 2 and 3 hop acres; 3 (6%) growing between 3 and 4 hop acres and 1 (2%) whose acreage is shown to have increased from 6 hop acres to 8 hop acres between 1658 and 1659.

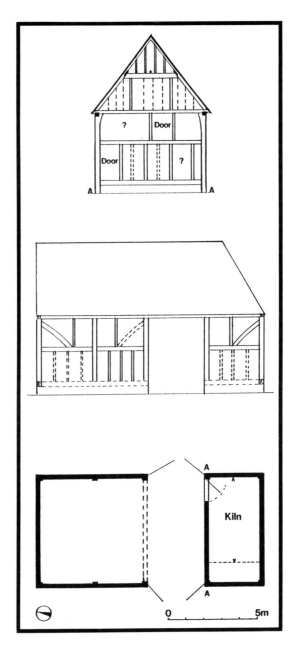

Fig. 9 Reconstruction Drawings of the plan, elevation and section of an early dual-purpose barn/oasthouse in Hawkhurst parish, Kent. The kiln is screened by a full-height partition. This and the vent (Fig. 11) marked a considerable technological advance in the seventeenth century.

16

Plantations of less than one hop acre Lord frequently referred to as 'spotts' rather than 'gardens' and many of those with 'spotts' were artisans rather than full-time farmers. Richard Harman the shoemaker, in arrears in 1647, owed '. . . . two michaelmasses for his hopps behind his house at the bridge foote and the little spotte on the side of the river. . . .' Such tradesmen are hardly likely to have had an oasthouse of their own; they are much more likely to have paid for the use of somebody else's. Even those farmers growing between one and two acres will not all have had a purpose-built oast; some will have used a dual-purpose building with a kiln incorporated into it. Several examples have been recorded.

One, in Hawkhurst, Kent, has a kiln at one end of a large barn which, to judge by its construction, dates from the late sixteenth or early seventeenth century. As one might expect, the drying-floor area, 2.95m. by 4.59m. (9 ft. 8 in. by 15 ft. 1 in.) was slightly greater than that of Scot's larger kiln, but there was no separate room for receiving the green hops and they must either have been left to cool on the kiln or shovelled down to the ground floor (Fig. 9).

Another example of the same period was recorded in Wartling parish, East Sussex, where a building, believed to have been used as a detached kitchen, later became an oasthouse with an inset kiln. Here again the area of the drying floor is greater, 3.05m. by 5.90m. (10 ft. by 19 ft. 4 in.). A partition was inserted to screen the kiln from the rest of the first floor which served for cooling and was slightly greater in area than the kiln itself.

Elsewhere maltkilns were made to serve a dual purpose. In the one shown in Fig. 8, which is dated 1652, two kilns inset within the building were used for drying both malt and hops. The dual use was proved when skirting boards in one kiln were removed during the conversion and an accumulation of hops and barley/oats was revealed.

There must have been many buildings adapted to hop drying in similar ways but, for the growers who were either richer or more specialist, purpose-built oasts were constructed. Some were still small. One, recorded by David and Barbara Martin, in Warbleton parish was a one-bay building with a lean-to.[10] Nevertheless, the drying floor, 3.77m. by 3.30m. (12 ft. 4 in. by 10 ft. 10 in.), was slightly larger than Scot's and in kiln area alone such seventeenth-century buildings were beginning to display considerable advance. This was to be increased yet again later in the century, as the Ticehurst oasthouses will show.

TABLE 2
16th.-and 17th.-century kiln areas compared

Parish	Area of kiln	Scot 1: % +	Scot 2: % +
Warbleton	3.77m. by 3.30m.	109%	67%
Hawkhurst	3.00m. by 4.60m.	132%	85%
Wartling	3.05m. by 5.90m.	202%	94%
Ticehurst	4.60m. by 4.60m.	251%	125%

[% + = percentage of increase in the area of the kiln compared with Scot's]

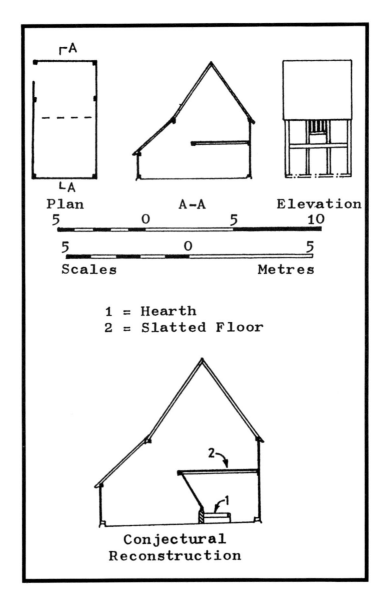

Fig. 10 A Seventeenth-century Oasthouse, Warbleton parish, East Sussex, which in size and function is comparable with both Scot's (Fig. 7) and that at Golford (Fig. 1). (*Drawing reproduced here by kind permission of David and Barbara Martin.*)

The Warbleton building is very similar to Scot's in that the drying floor was left open to the adjoining area and would have been loaded from a ladder; it is also clear from the blackened rafters that wood was burned and there is no evidence of a vent (Fig. 10). In the Wartling and Hawkhurst oasthouses, however, other advances in technique over Scot are recognisable. A pair of rafters were truncated just below the apex and a vent was opened (Fig. 11). Neither roof bore any trace of soot blackening, indicating that charcoal or some other smokeless fuel had been used and this would have resulted in a better quality product. In addition, the partition dividing the kiln from the adjoining area on the first floor was taken right up to the roof. In conjunction with the vent this not only would have improved the air flow, but, particularly important where kilns had been incorporated into barns, would have increased the quality of the final product while protecting the other crops stored in the rest of the building. The demerits of these buildings are their lack of provision for receiving the green hops and with one exception, their lack of a cooling floor.

As the century progressed, the richer tenants and owner-occupiers who farmed land with suitable soil, invested ever more heavily in hops. This phenomenon was already visible in Lord's *Tithe Book*: John Fowle with his six acres was already cultivating twice or three times as many as most of his rivals even before his increase to eight acres.[11] For such men a specialist building must soon have become necessary, and as they were built, each one would embody all the known advances in the art of drying. Some idea of the cost, layout and technological advance of each one is conveyed by documents which fortunately survive for three buildings.

Fig. 11 A Kiln Vent, the former position of which is indicated by the truncated rafters. Hawkhurst parish, Kent.

19

For the first, built in Flimwell, Ticehurst parish, East Sussex, in 1667, an agreement was drawn up between the landowner Walter Roberts, his tenant Thomas Hovenden and two carpenters, John Hodge (variably spelt Hoadge) and John Buss (variably spelt Buse)[12] (Fig. 12). Translated into modern English it reads:

'Firstly the said Walter is to fell sufficient rough timber or timber to build one oasthouse at Flimwell on the land which Thomas Hovenden occupies and it is to be built thirty foot in length and fifteen foot in breadth (4.57m. by 9.14m.) and he is to pay them three shillings a foot, based on the measurement of one wall along the building and one across, neither to exceed the stated measurements. Secondly, the said John Hodge and John Buss are to make three doors, and stairs, and a partition between the chamber and oast; and they are to do all the carpentry work necessary for the building, whose posts are to measure ten foot (3.04m.) between the sill and the wall plate, and no more. And they are to fell the timber where I tell them to and they are to finish the work between this day, August 6th. 1667, and the 20th. November next. To this document we the undersigned

John Hodge

John Buss

do set our hands.

And the said Thomas Hovenden has agreed to give them one rib of beef and a kilderkin* of beer at the rearing, when the frame is put up, and likewise is to fetch all the loam which shall be used about the oasthouse'.

This building has a partition specified and since only one is mentioned, this presumably indicates a division of the building into two areas: kiln and stowage. Once again there was no separate provision for the green hops. In area the kiln probably matched, possibly exceeded that of the Hawkhurst kiln but the building was not so tall. No mention is made of a vent. Four years later, however, the same owner and carpenter were agreeing the specifications for another oast:[13]

'Bargained with John Russ the carpenter to build me one oasthouse with two kilns to be thirty two foot (9.76m.) in length and sixteen or seventeen foot (4.88m. or 5.18m.) in breadth and the post to be ten foot (3.04m.) between the sill and the wall-plate and one outlet (vent) at two pence the foot and he is to measure one head and one side of the oasthouse and the outlet and I am to pay him three shillings the foot for the oasthouse and two pence the foot for the outlet and no more for which sums he is to do all manner of carpenters work to fell timber and hew for the several uses that is for boards for the chambers and for the kilns and partitions and stairs and windows and all other things necessary to the building for the several uses and the said John Buss doth engage to render it by the twentieth of May next coming and to complete his work that the mason may go to work. Dated the sixteenth day of February 1671'.

There are a number of important details included here:

a) There was an overall increase of 14% in the area.

b) The document speaks of two kilns but does not specify the way the word 'kel' was being used. It could mean kiln as we understand it today but could also be used to mean 'furnace'.[14] If the meaning intended was 'kilns' then this would reflect the need for extra drying space following the increase in the hop acreage apparent in other entries in the book and it would seem that two

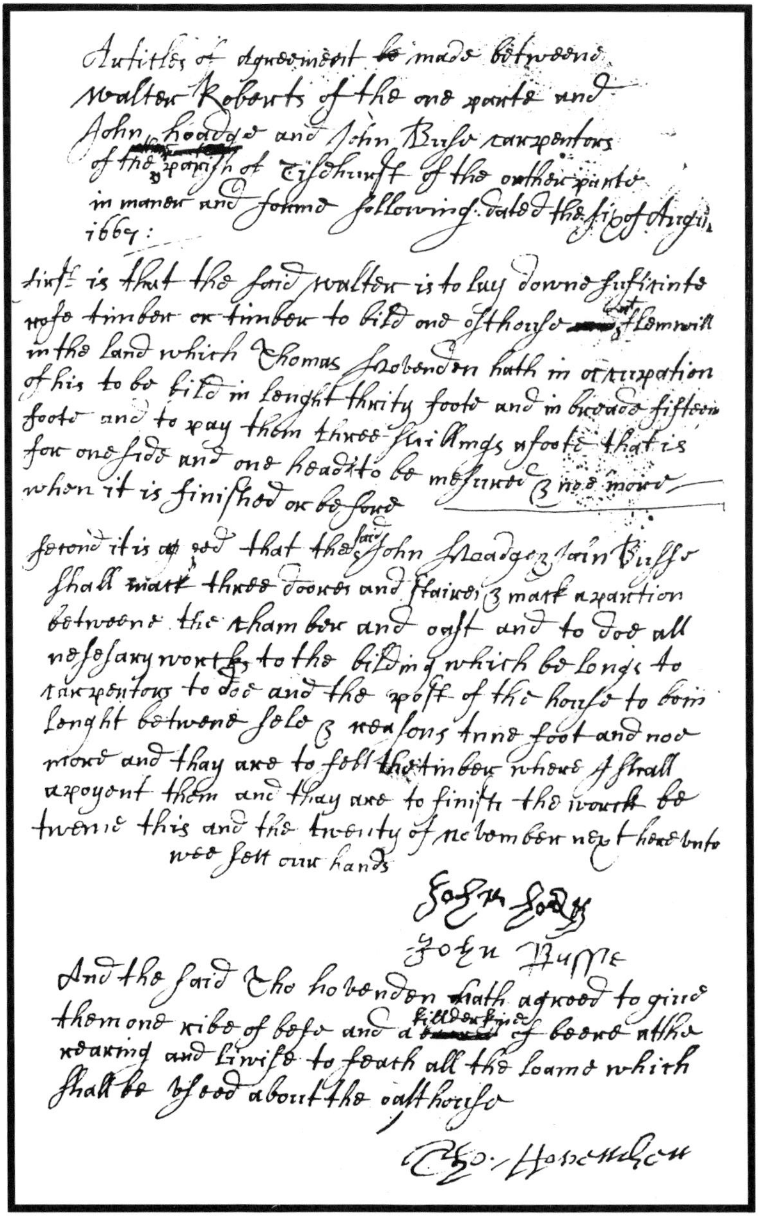

Artitles of agreement to made betweene
Walter Roberts of the one parte and
John Headge and John Buss carpentors
of the parish of Tisehurst of the other parte
in maner and forme following dated the fift of April
1667:

First is that the said Walter is to lay downe suffitiente
rofe timber or timber to bild one osthouse at Flemwell
in the land which Thomas Hovenden hath in occupation
of his to be bild in lenght thirty foote and in breade fifteen
foote and to pay them three shillings a foote that is
for one side and one head to be mesured & noe more
when it is finished or before

Second it is agreed that the said John Headge & John Busse
shall make three doores and staires & make a partition
betweene the chamber and ost and to doe all
nesesary worke to the bilding which belongs to
carpentors to doe and the post of the house to bee
lenght betweene sole & reasons nine foot and noe
more and thay are to fell the timber where I shall
appoynt them and thay are to finish the worke be
tweene this and the twenty of november next heare unto
wee sett our hands

John Hedge
John Busse

And the said Tho Hovenden hath agreed to give
them one ribe of befe and a kilderkin of beere at the
rearing and lirise to fetch all the loame which
shall be used about the osthouse

Tho: Hovenden

Fig. 12 An Agreement between landowner, tenant farmer and carpenters to build an oasthouse on a farm belonging to the Boarzell Estate, East Sussex in 1667. (*The document is deposited in the East Sussex Record Office and is reproduced here by kind permission of Mr. P.H.Dunn.*)

separate kilns were required. If 'kel' was used to mean 'furnace', then it is possible that only one large kiln heated by two furnaces was intended. Both interpretations are possible, the latter seeming perhaps more likely in view of the fact that only one vent was envisaged.

c) This is the first document actually to specify the framing of an outlet but we know from the same account book that one was inserted into Boarzell oasthouse in 1666, so clearly they had been used for some time.

The third building agreement specified further advances in overall area - it was to be 16 ft. by 36 ft. (4.87m. by 10.97m.) and, significantly perhaps, note is made that it was to be sufficiently strong to bear tiling, making the building much more fire-resistant. Tile was expensive and most oasthouses, in common with other farm buildings, were thatched.[15]

The general outline of the development through the seventeenth century seems clear: with variations dependent sometimes on farm size, and always on soil and available capital, the size of the buildings and of the individual kilns increased to keep pace with the increase in hop acreages. Cooling floors were omitted in some, provided in others, but perhaps because many buildings were adapted, perhaps for reasons of economy or shortage of space, provision for the green hops seems often to have been forgotten. Chimneys or vents were eventually recognised as necessary.

A very rough idea of the cost of these buildings is provided by the sum of £ 30 3s. 2d. (£ 30.16) which is quoted as having been paid for the labour and material on the building put up in 1667. It does not include the cost of the timber, most of which came from the Estate. The provision for felling and hewing makes it clear that most of the timber used was new. Just occasionally older trusses were re-used - Goodman Sone was paid £ 2 12s. 6d. (£ 2.63) for four pieces of frame - but the outlay was large, a reflection, perhaps, of the importance of the crop.

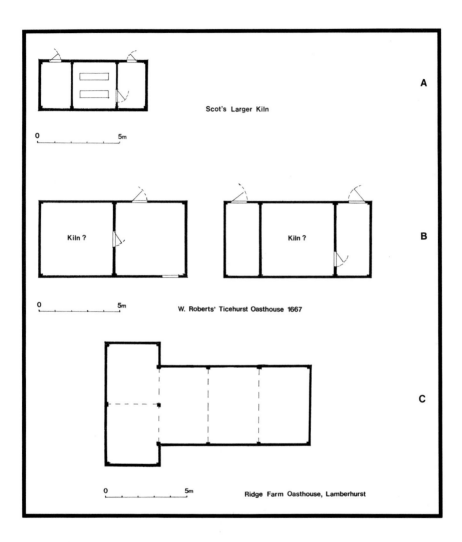

Fig. 13 The Development in Oasthouse Size between the late sixteenth and the early eighteenth centuries is indicated by the oasthouses represented above. The kilns B and C are of similar size - C being only 10% greater in area than B. Both represent an increase in area of more than 100% over the Scot kiln of the late sixteenth century.

23

CHAPTER 4
Hops Become an Industry

'. . . . the Hop, which considering the small space of Ground it takes up, in comparison to other Plants, and small Expence of Planting, the prodigious Profit to the Proportion, and the great Advantage it brings to the Crown of Great Britain, is well worth our consideration.'

(Richard Bradley, 1729)[16]

Assuming that the building of three new oasthouses and the renovation of another on one small estate is probably typical of many other estates, it could be thought that 'consideration' had already been fairly generously given to hop growing during the seventeenth century (Fig. 13). Even in 1652, hops had been said to have been 'grown to a Nationall Commodity' as the demand for beer spread into the countryside where conservative opposition had persisted longest.[17]

Bradley's recommendation therefore seems to invite the conclusion that demand was still outstripping supply and this is supported by the fact that in 1690 the Government imposed an import duty of 20s. (£ 1) per cwt. (50.8kg.) on foreign hops, further increasing it to 28s. (£ 1.40) in 1710. This offered the English farmer some protection against foreign competition and brought much needed revenue to the Exchequer. The fact that two Acts were passed implies that the levels of imports were significant, due, perhaps, to a growing popular preference for porter - a thick, strong dark beer for which a greater proportion of hops was used.[18]

Like Scot before him, Bradley, in his desire to encourage hop growing, made his introductory remarks rather over-optimistic:

'For even Ground that was never before esteemed worth a shilling per Acre per Annum, is rendered worth forty, fifty or sometimes more Pounds a year'.[19]

Small wonder then that with such encouragement, in important hop-growing parishes expanding hop acreages created the need for larger buildings. As an example of this, an oasthouse in Lamberhurst known to have been in position in 1750 shows the scale of increase which had taken place in some areas by the first half of the eighteenth century. It was originally entirely timber-framed under a tiled roof in the direct tradition of oasthouse building as we have seen it develop during the seventeenth century. It embodied a number of improvements which testify to the growing expertise and understanding of the farmers of the day: the building was 'T' shaped and the kiln, situated in the top of the 'T', was considerably larger, 6.95m. by 3.33m. (7 ft. 7 in. by 3 ft. 7 in.), and had a central chimney at the ridge.[20] This design appears to have become increasingly popular during the eighteenth century, probably because it made loading and unloading the hops for drying and cooling easier than they would have been in a long building (Fig. 14). The cooling floor, which over time had become much larger than that provided in the sixteenth century, was here equal in area to that of the kiln and was lined with boarding to keep the hops clean. The windows

24

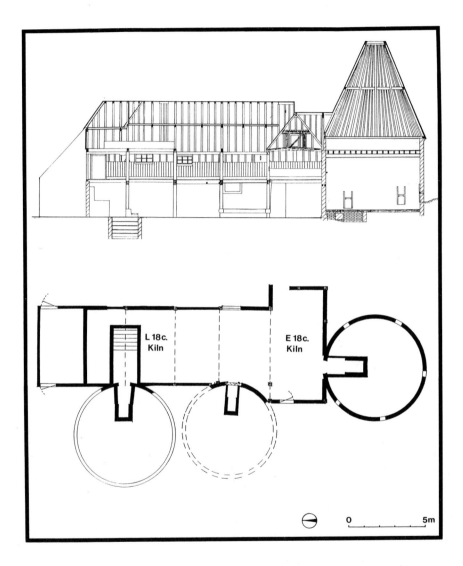

Fig. 14 An Early Eighteenth-century, 'T'-shaped, Timber-Framed Oasthouse (depicted in Fig. 13C), Lamberhurst parish, Kent, probably initially used for malting also, had by the end of the eighteenth century become inadequate, because of the increase in hop acreage, and the building was enlarged at the north end by the addition of a bay and a lean-to. The original end bay was then converted into an extra kiln. Four more alterations were to be made in the nineteenth and twentieth centuries.

25

had sliding shutters in order to keep out unwanted draught and excessive sunlight.

Among the growers, understanding of the importance of the cooling floor was slowly spreading, probably precisely because hop acreages were rising: any grower wishing to put more fields down to hops must have found that without a cooling floor the limitations on the quantity of hops which could be properly cooled, inevitably restricted any increase to a minimum. Therefore, where the age or the small scale of existing buildings made addition and extension impossible, new oasthouses were provided. On smaller farms, or in less important hop-growing areas where acreage increase was minimal, the old buildings remained in use for much of the century.

Another oasthouse which stands near a tributary of the eastern Rother in Mayfield parish embodies similar progress (Fig. 15). This building is probably of mid-eighteenth-century date and served a farm of 186 acres in a parish where moderate acreages of hops were grown on many farms.[21] Again entirely timber-framed under a tiled roof, this oasthouse is rectangular in plan. The original kiln, situated at one end of the building, was rectangular, and measured 5.65m. by 4.5m. (18 ft. 6 in. by 14 ft. 9 in.). Its area, 27.84m². (273 sq. ft.) was therefore slightly greater than that of the kiln in the Lamberhurst oasthouse. Above the level of the drying floor the top of the kiln is formed into an inverted funnel. This is made by framing, within the roof space, secondary walls of lath and plaster which terminate in the chimney in the ridge. The tie-beam across the centre of the kiln is quite sharply cambered in order to give the men loading the hops more headroom. Similar attention was paid to headroom when the cooling floor was planned: the truncated tie-beam framing allows complete freedom of movement along the cooling floor; its trusses were put into the building new and are all numbered in sequence. A treading hole framed into one of the corners furthest from the kiln ensured that the hops moved progressively through the building. In the roof and elsewhere in the building there was considerable re-use of timber reflecting either the growing scarcity of building timber, or a natural desire for economy on the part of the landowner who provided the building. The re-use of timber necessitated two bays of staggered butt-purlin* roof where old rafters which were too short for the new roof were cut and framed into the purlins.

Owing to later alteration, and in spite of having excavated the floor of the Lamberhurst oasthouse, we do not know what method of firing was originally used in either of these buildings. Nevertheless, it seems reasonable to conclude that they represent a considerable improvement in drying methods when compared to the small, inconvenient buildings where hops cooled in the kiln and were then thrown down to the ground floor for packing.

But it is already clear that not all eighteenth-century oasthouses necessarily embodied such advances. Then, as always, provision of buildings depended on the acreage; their quality depended on the availability of capital and on the level of investment in hops. Throughout the century numerous small growers struggled to make a profit out of small hop acreages. Some of them only entered the market when profits were high and left it when they were low. To judge by a few surviving examples, the oasthouses provided for them were largely contrived out of existing and sometimes redundant buildings.

Fig. 15   An Eighteenth-century Oasthouse in Mayfield parish, East Sussex, which survives with some later additions to the kiln. The use of truncated tie-beam trusses allowed freedom of movement on the cooling floor.

A particularly good example stands in Sutton Valence parish, Kent, on what was a smallholding of 8.09 ha. (20 acres). This building has three walls largely constructed of timber re-used from a mediaeval house. One wall of that house together with its diamond-mullioned window* actually survives as part of one of the oasthouse walls. The stretch which included the mediaeval window served as one wall of the kiln with the window covered by a layer of lath and plaster. Brick was used for the remaining two outside walls of the kiln but timber partitions were provided to separate it from the rest of the building (Fig. 16). Just how much of the land was under hops is not known but it seems unlikely that the kiln inset at the end of the building could have dried more than 1.62 ha. (4 acres) - an acreage typical of many farms in many parishes at the end of the eighteenth century.

It is surprising, then, to find the author of a tract published in 1733 to encourage Irish farmers to take up hop cultivation, saying:

'Tis common *in England* to see ten, twenty, or thirty Acres of Hops, or more, in the Hands of one Man, and some receive 2000 l. a Year for their Hops, notwithstanding the high Price of Labour, Manure, and of every other Article relating to the Management of Hops. But then no Care, Industry or Expence is wanting to make their Plantations flourish'. [22]

While such acreages certainly existed in the specialist areas of Kent, which even then was foremost in growing hops, whether they were 'common' is more doubtful and even there many farmers still had less than 4.05 ha. (10 acres). A more normal picture is revealed in Table 3 where the figures are taken from the Tithe records for the parish of Ewhurst in East Sussex.

TABLE 3
Acreages of Hops from 1760-1771

Acres	Years 1760 - 1771												
	60	61	62	63	64	65	66	67	68	69	70	71	Overall
0<1	2	3	3	5	3	2	2	2	1	1	2	3	29
1<2	5	3	4	2	6	5	5	5	5	3	3	3	49
2<3	4	2	2	2	1	2	4	3	3	4	3	3	33
3<4	3	4	2	4	3	4	4	3	4	2	4	2	39
4<5	2	3	4	3	4	3	2	4	2	4	3	3	37
5<6	1	0	1	0	0	0	0	0	1	0	0	2	5
6<7	0	1	0	1	1	1	1	0	0	0	1	1	7
7<8	0	1	2	1	2	1	0	1	0	0	0	1	9
9<10	1	1	0	1	0	0	0	0	0	1	0	0	4
10<11	0	0	0	1	0	0	0	0	1	0	0	1	4
11<12	2	2	2	1	1	0	0	1	1	0	1	0	11
12<13	1	0	0	0	0	0	1	0	1	1	2	1	7
13<14	0	0	0	0	0	0	0	1	1	1	0	0	3
14<15	0	0	0	0	1	1	1	0	0	1	0	1	5
15<16	0	0	0	0	0	0	0	0	0	0	1	1	2
Farms	22	21	21	22	23	21	22	23	21	20	21	23	260

Source: E.S.R.O. PAR 364/1/6

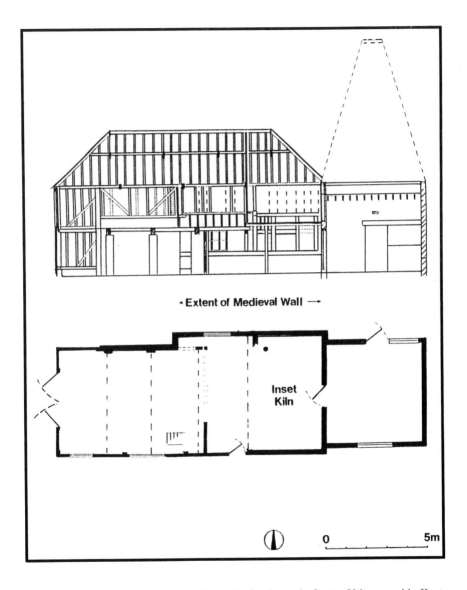

Extent of Medieval Wall →

Inset
Kiln

0   5m

Fig. 16   An Eighteenth-century Smallholder's Oasthouse in Sutton Valence parish, Kent incorporates part of a medieval house and a great deal of medieval timber. It is a good example of the re-use of existing buildings, commonly made during this period of agricultural depression on farms where the hop acreage was only moderate.

29

It can be seen that over twelve years, 58% of the acreages given show cultivation of less than 4 acres, 28% between 4 and 9 acres, 11% between 9 and 14 acres and 3% of over 14 acres. No farmer was cultivating 20 acres and the rise above 14 acres comes only in and after 1764 at a time when the birthrate began to increase throughout England. The population was to continue rising right into the second half of the nineteenth century with the result that demand for beer increased. As this happened, it stimulated extra production, necessarily increasing the demand for hops. Map and field evidence shows that during the last quarter of the eighteenth century further kilns were added to existing oasthouses or new oasthouses were built with greater kiln space. Some of these new kilns became very large indeed.

Another kiln was added at this time to the Lamberhurst oasthouse described above; two other oasthouses in Ewhurst parish itself serve as good examples of these changes (Figs. 17 & 18). That in Figure 17 served a small farm of roughly 18.21 ha. (45 acres) and as originally built was a small two-bay timber-framed building in which there was a small kiln 3.21m. by 4.32m. (10 ft. 6 in. by 14 ft. 2 in.) which might have dried about 0.81 ha. (2 acres) of hops. A hatch like the one described in Scot allowed the dried hops to be shovelled down into the adjacent lean-to for packing.

Two bays were added, one at each end. Both were timber-framed, and were probably separate undertakings. In the first the drying floor was extended and another hatch was added; in the second the building was extended sufficiently for the kiln to be transferred to the other end. The drying floor was raised in height and a cowled vent was made in the ridge. As a result of these 'improvements' this building remained in use for nearly three quarters of the nineteenth century until it was replaced in 1873.

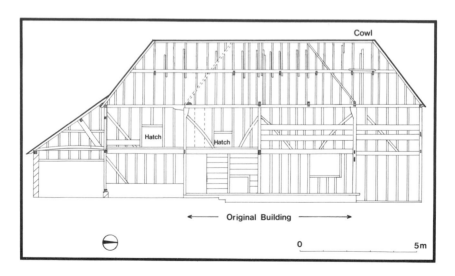

Fig. 17   An Eighteenth-century Oasthouse Extended, Ewhurst parish, East Sussex. Here the original two-bay oasthouse, still clearly identifiable in the timberwork, was subsequently enlarged by additions, first at the south end and then at the north.

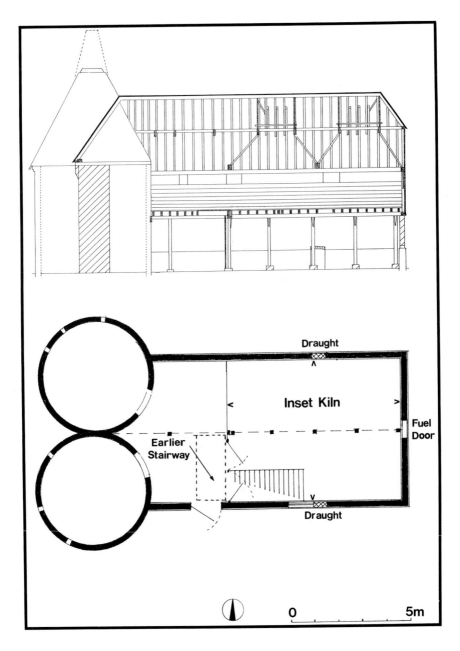

Fig. 18 Late Eighteenth-century Oasthouse, with inset kiln and two later roundels, Ewhurst parish, East Sussex. Excavation has shown that this large area was used as one kiln and this conclusion is corroborated by the position of the draught openings. Such a large kiln is typical of a period when hop acreages were increasing steadily.

31

That in Figure 18, built towards the end of the eighteenth century, served a farm of about 24.28 ha. (60 acres) and was built of brick on the ground floor but was timber-framed and weatherboarded on the first floor. It was purpose-built as an oasthouse and typical of the period in that it contained one very large kiln, 6.00m. by 7.10m. (19 ft 8 in. by 23 ft. 3 in.). This kiln was subdivided on the first floor. Each half had the familiar inverted funnel framed up into the roof and terminated in a chimney surmounted by a cowl. A treading hole was framed into the floor at the south-west corner but either the hops were left to cool on the drying floor or they were not laid very thickly on it because the floor space at this end of the building is roughly half the area of that of the kiln. A partition probably screened the kiln on the ground floor. Here there was no subdivision within the kiln itself: the position of the draught openings indicates that the firing must have been central, serving both halves of the kiln. When the floor was excavated prior to redevelopment of the building, it was surprising not to find in the centre any trace of permanent structures which could have housed the fires. Instead, two depressions were found. These had a hard top layer of burnt clay 25-30mm. (1 in. to 1^1/4 in.) thick in which pieces or short lengths of charcoal were embedded. This suggested that the fires may have been set in removable braziers (known to have been used on some farms) or even on the ground itself.[23]

Whereas this oasthouse was only partially built in brick which was more expensive than timber, during the second half of the century many more were built entirely in brick, particularly on farms owned by wealthy landlords. On the Ashburnham estate, for example, where timber remained plentiful but which also had its own brickyards, brick was increasingly used when the farm buildings were rebuilt or replaced. Eventually it became impossible to continue enlarging the kiln-space inside the buildings and gradually brick or stone kilns were built outside, either at the end or alongside. This was a logical extension of the arrangement of the kilns in a T-shaped oasthouse and it is the great innovation of the eighteenth century. Marshall mentions one oasthouse in Maidstone which had ten kilns and those which survive at Sissinghurst Castle Farm are also believed to be of this date.[24] Six others, now lost, formerly stood appended to a building dated 1796 at Swarling Manor near Petham in Kent. Kilns like these must have answered or obviated the problems posed by the very large kilns where it must often have been very difficult to maintain constant levels of heat.

As usual, the new ideas spread slowly and rather unevenly. The very large kilns continued to find favour with some growers and were still being built in the nineteenth century. The problems they posed were finally either solved or swept away by the experiments and innovations brought into being by the new century's more scientific approach to agriculture.

CHAPTER 5
The Nineteenth Century - A Ferment of Activity

The more scientific approach was stimulated by the social and economic changes of the times: the Industrial Revolution had encouraged enquiry and experiment at the same time as the rise in the population brought the prospect of poverty and famine. The economic situation was complicated by the Napoleonic wars which impeded importation. Landlords and farmers strove to increase production in order to offset shortages, and this itself stimulated experiment paid for by a temporary boom in market prices while imports were restricted.

The pace of change slackened when prices fell sharply after the end of the war, thus curtailing the amount of money available for improvements. Depression continued through the 1820s as poor seasons added to the difficulties and, as a result, the burdens of Poor Rates* and Tithes grew heavier. Only towards the end of the 1830s did the tide turn and bring prosperity back during the 1840s. With capital once more available, rebuilding began again in earnest on many farms giving oasthouses their now familiar shapes.

This revolution had started at the end of the eighteenth century when the need to increase production had encouraged experiment with very large external kilns. These, however, had aggravated the familiar problems of hop drying. A good example is the large kiln, 6.57m. by 4.21m. (21 ft. 6 in. by 13 ft. 10 in.), brick-built on a substantial stone plinth and with a tiled roof, which was added to a timber-framed malthouse in Ashburnham parish. The malt-kiln, 2.9m. by 4.82m. (9 ft. 6 in. by 15 ft. 10 in.) had sufficed for drying both malt and hops since at least 1721 when the building is first mentioned in an inventory, and the stone and brick kiln was probably added to its northern end in 1813 when the Ashburnham Estate Accounts show an expenditure of £ 64 on the farm buildings (Fig. 19).[25] (The price compares well with the £ 164 known to have been estimated for a new brick-built oasthouse for which the plans survive in the Battle Abbey archives, see below). An Estate Survey of 1830 tells us that the Ashburnham kiln had six fireplaces.[26] Not only must it have been very expensive to heat, but once the required temperature was reached it can only have been maintained with difficulty when humidity levels were high or when the wind was slack. In addition, there was the danger that more fireplaces would bring an increase in noxious gases produced naturally by the fuel.

The solving of problems with contamination had right from the beginning of the hop industry encouraged experimentation.[27] Enclosed stoves from which the combustion products escaped *via* pipework taken through the external wall are said to have been introduced as an experiment during the 1740s, and simple versions were in use on some farms by the 1790s.[28] They, while solving some of the problems, aggravated others or presented new ones: variations in temperature were more difficult to rectify quickly and installation was more expensive. Many growers, therefore, taking as much care as possible to avoid

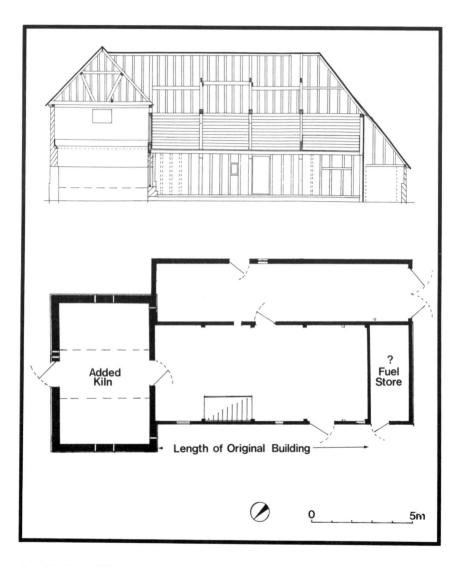

Fig. 19 Early Nineteenth-century Kiln, added to an eighteenth-century Malthouse, Ashburnham parish, East Sussex. Added during the boom-time of the Napoleonic Wars, the kiln was large. It was constructed of brick on a stone plinth, although the malthouse itself was timber-framed.

34

contaminating the hops, still preferred to work with the old-fashioned open grates because with them they could see and judge what was happening more easily.

Nevertheless, John Read of Horsmonden, a gardener and inventor with wide experience of greenhouse horticulture, began to experiment with improvements to hop kilns in about 1796. Over the first quarter of the nineteenth century he perfected a system which derived both from the early stoves and from the heating used in greenhouses. His plans were published by J. C. Loudon in his *Encyclopaedia* of 1833 and enthusiastically reviewed by him (Fig. 20).[29] He had adopted a new circular form and had devised a very elaborate scheme for carrying heated air up towards the drying floor. The circular shape offered strength, space and economy in outlay:

'*The circular form* for the kiln has been adopted by Mr. Read, because it contains a greater area than any other figure with the same quantity of exterior walling; and because both the walls and roof can be made stronger than they can in any rectangular form, with fewer materials. Hence, while the circular kilns possess more strength and durability than the rectangular ones, the expense of construction is less'.

The new oasthouses married function and form very aesthetically and they are still much prized for the charm which they add to the landscape. The installations described by Loudon were expensive, however. The four kilns illustrated cost £ 700 and even allowing for some inflation in the first quarter of the century, that sum has to be compared with the £ 64 known to have been spent in Ashburnham where only the kiln was added, and with £ 164 quoted as the estimated cost for the new oasthouse built in Battle parish. Clearly the new technological roundels were investments that only rich and entrepreneurial growers or landowners would afford.

There were many of them, however, and many such roundels were built. Thomas Daws, a Sussex grower from Ewhurst, had 67.99 ha. (168 acres) of hops in 1835.[30] Four kilns of this design are known from diary evidence to have been installed on one of his farms after the existing oasthouse burnt down:[31]

'Dreadful fire at Shoreham oast house Barn and 3 lodges burnt'. (Thomas Daws. 24/9/1830).

'Mr. John Reed (*sic*) here to draw the plan of the new built barn at Shoreham. New plan of new oast house at Shoreham'. (Thomas Daws. 31/5/1831).

'Seting out Oast Shoreham with Mr. John Reed'. (Thomas Chester Daws. 31/1/1831).

'Mr. Selmes and Mr. Langford dined - they approved of my new oast house at Shoreham'. (Thomas Chester Daws. 22/9/1831) [32] (Fig. 21).

Not only was this new oasthouse built. The diary of Thomas Daws mentions another on one of his other farms, which replaced an oasthouse built only in 1808:

'New oast at Madamse's dries very well'. (Thomas Daws. 23/9/1830).

By the time the Tithe Map was produced in 1843, they had had another four-kiln oast (now demolished) built at Padgham farm and this may also have been to identical specifications. Yet another, with a date of 1845 and bearing the name of Thomas Chester Daws was built at Lording Court Farm. All four roundels had external flues but here all four kilns were of the same dimension.

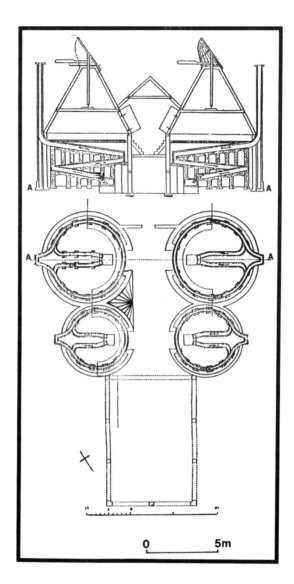

0   5m

Fig. 20 The Plan and Sections of John Read's Roundels. They were published in Loudon's *Encyclopaedia* in 1833. Much thought had been put into these designs. Round kilns were economic in their use of brick. The variation in the size of the kiln allowed for small loads at the end of the day or during wet seasons. The enclosed firing and stove-pipe venting ensured that the hops would be free from contamination due to combustion products. The pipes which carried the heat up close to the drying floor were designed to ensure even drying right across the drying floor, with no cold spots. Economic dual use was ensured by the cart shed beneath the cooling floor and this also contributed to good, even cooling. Nevertheless, at £ 700 these were expensive buildings.

36

Fig. 21 Shoreham Oasthouse, Kent. Built with four kilns, only two roundels survive, but this oast has historic importance in that it is known to have been designed by John Reed.

Such investment typified the larger hop growers but could hardly be emulated by the smaller ones. Authorities on hop drying had quickly commented on the absence of 'cold corners' in the new-shaped kilns and poorer or less committed growers or landowners wished to copy the kilns while seeking in various ways to cut down the expenditure involved.[33]

Some, therefore, copied only the shape and retained traditional open grates screened by firing tunnels or inner circles.[34] Others copied the technology of the kilns as well, but contented themselves with adding them to existing stowages. Others again found less expensive ways of carrying the pipes up towards the drying floor than by the brick columns advocated by Read. In Lamberhurst parish for example, the solution adopted by a local kiln-builder has been identified on several farms: the pipes were carried on a series of sandstone 'brackets' which were built into the kiln walls (Fig. 22). With the adoption of solutions like these, increasing numbers of roundels were built in Kent and Sussex as the capacity of the older oasthouses was found to be inadequate. In these two counties particularly, roundels were built right up to the end of the nineteenth century and just a few were built in the twentieth.

Since acreages continued to increase into the 1860s and remained at a high level until the 1880s, the capacities of the kilns had to be stretched as far as possible and one way of doing this was to increase the draught of hot air through the hops. It was found that this could be done by raising the height of the cone, which pulled the hot air up through the kiln more quickly. As a result the kilns

37

Fig. 22 A Ruinous Oasthouse in Horsmonden parish, Kent. Sandstone Brackets in the wall of the kiln are seen rising from left to right below the mortices for the drying-floor joists. These were a cheaper alternative to the brickwork used by Read to carry the pipes in his kilns. This was evidently an economic design employed by a local builder in the Lamberhurst/ Hawkhurst area, where several examples of the use of sandstone brackets have been recorded. They show that even a ruinous building can reveal significant details.

got progressively taller as the century wore on, although for other reasons this development was reversed in the twentieth century.

The other main development was in the construction itself. When first introduced the kilns were usually built one-brick thick to eaves level with the rafters of the cone rising up to the curb of the cowl opening, from a circular plate on top of the wall. These rafters were then lathed and plastered internally and tiled externally with specially shaped 'oast tiles'. From about the middle of the century the cones were also built of brick, half-brick thick. These needed no plastering internally and were rendered to make them weather-proof externally (Fig. 23). Gradually, other materials were also introduced: stone for the kiln walls and slate for some roofs.

Later, there was a general return to more 'traditional' square kilns, claims of even drying and no 'cold corners' having been found to belong more to legend than to fact. It would be wrong, however, to suppose that this decision came everywhere at the end of the century. In some counties, notably Surrey, Herefordshire, Worcestershire and Hampshire, the roundel was much less widely adopted and even in Kent and Sussex there were those who held out against it. Square or rectangular kilns persisted and slightly different lines of enquiry and experiment were pursued in order to increase their performance and capacity.

38

Fig. 23 Conical Roof Construction. The cone in the top photograph continues the traditional use of timber, lath and plaster, and tile, although the tiles for this type of roof had to be specially tapered. After the removal of the brick tax the cones were constructed entirely of brick, as in the lower photograph. The cross-piece which supported the pivot of the cowl therefore had to be built into the brickwork.

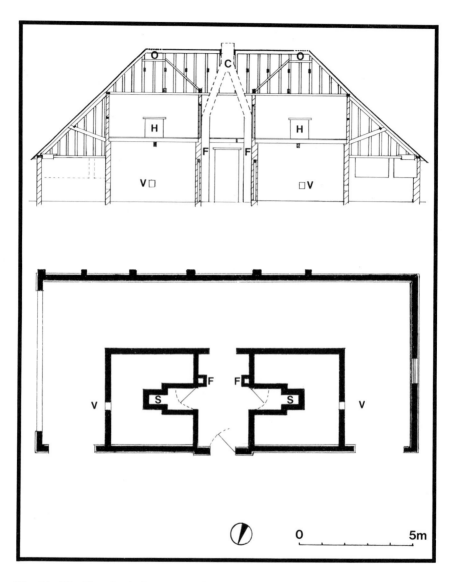

Fig. 24 The First Lord Carrington's Oasthouse. This oasthouse was built in 1827 in Mayfield parish, East Sussex, and is an important example of the continuing use of inset kilns. Vents (V) supplied draught to the stoves (S) and pipes took the combustion products into the flues (F) of a central chimney (C). During the drying the hot air escaped from the kiln through openings (O) in the ridge of the roof. When dry the hops were removed from the kiln through hatches (H), reminiscent of those in the earliest kilns, and then cooled, pressed and stored in the lean-to. The reconstruction drawing is based on excavation.

Surprisingly, even while external kilns and enclosed stoves and finally roundels were being more widely introduced, the traditional, 'old-fashioned' inset kilns were still being built on some farms. The plans for one built in 1814 survive in the Battle Abbey archive, proving how uneven was the spread of new ideas.[35] On some farms inset kilns were still being built with traditional firing in the second decade of the nineteenth century. On others, however, enclosed stoves were adopted for them and the design of oasthouses with inset kilns developed considerably. One, built in 1827 on a farm which had been bought in 1823 by Robert, Lord Carrington, had two such kilns in a very carefully designed building which had an unusually graceful facade (Fig. 24). The two flue pipes which were removed during later improvements probably terminated in a central chimney. There was a vent constructed in the ridge of each kiln as an outlet for the hot air but lack of evidence for a pivot support makes it uncertain whether they were ever surmounted by a cowl.

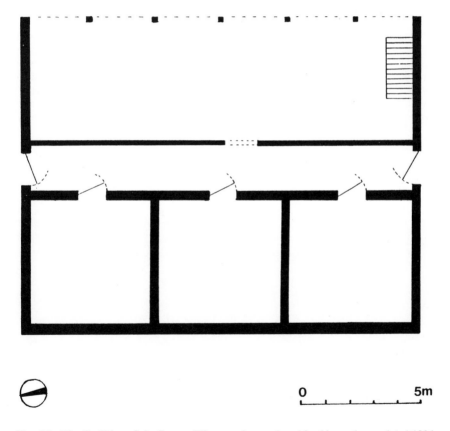

0 _____ 5m

Fig. 25   The Tradition of the Square Kiln was also continued in this oasthouse dated 1834 in Salehurst parish, East Sussex. Here the kilns had tall pyramidal roofs. Access to them was from a corridor, on the other side of which was a large cooling floor, constructed over a wagon shed.

41

In their firing these kilns must have seemed very up-to-date while to us, their lack of a separate cooling floor seems curiously out-of-date. The hops must either have dried on these kilns and then been 'scuppeted'* down to the floor of the surrounding lean-to for packing, or else have been 'scuppeted' straight down for cooling, which would have caused some damage and loss of resin. The hatches built into the kiln walls for this purpose are direct descendants of the hatch shown in later editions of Scot. Similar hatches and lean-tos have been recorded on farms on the Ashburnham Estate. They suggest that the finer points of cooling and pressing were, on some farms at least, still to be appreciated.

On others, they already were. An oasthouse built in Salehurst parish, East Sussex, and dated 1834, has three external square kilns served by a large cooling floor (Fig. 25). A similar plan was adopted by a builder named Hards for an oasthouse built in 1830 in Nettlestead parish, Kent, and here there was intelligent provision of a smaller kiln in order to avoid waste of time and fuel when only small amounts of hops needed to be dried (Fig. 26). All the elements in these two plans readily admitted the possibility of enlarging the kiln space: the building merely needed to be longer for it to include more kilns.

Loudon published the plan for a similar oasthouse with three kilns, each fired by two traditional honeycombed brick furnaces (Fig. 27).[36] As can be seen from his detailed illustrations, the provision of draught was very carefully considered: each kiln had two draught openings low in the rear wall while fresh air was also ducted through pipes and vents in the brick pavement surrounding the furnaces. Furthermore, this oasthouse made provision for two drying floors, one above the other. The aim was no doubt one of economy, but in practice many driers

Fig. 26 Oasthouse dated 1830, Nettlestead parish, Kent. Here a similar plan was adopted. The important difference is that the three kilns to the right and centre of the photograph, two large and one smaller, were built inset. Another inset kiln was later added alongside and finally an external square kiln was built at the end.

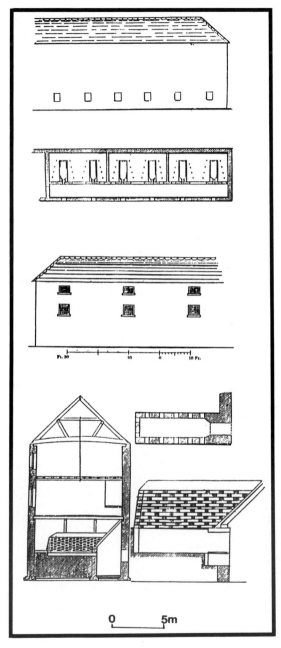

Fig. 27 An Oasthouse from Farnham, Surrey. Published by Loudon in 1833, it has obvious similarities with the Nettlestead oasthouse shown in Fig. 26.

43

appear to have found that moisture-laden air failed to penetrate and pass through the upper floor. In consequence the use of the two drying floors was often discontinued.

A plan for a similar but more elaborate building was published twenty years later in Morton's *Cyclopaedia of Agriculture*.[37] The upper drying floor was omitted and a series of arched openings on the ground floor provided a fuel store adjacent to each kiln. Both designs incorporated vent openings in the roof rather than cowls, but in the one example of this design recorded so far, these openings had been found to be inadequate and two chimney openings, not dissimilar to those of the seventeenth century had been inserted at the ridge (Fig. 28).

The square or rectangular kiln can therefore be seen to have undergone its own separate evolution although it is far from clear how many of this type of oasthouse were built in Kent and Sussex. Visits to Hampshire, Surrey, Herefordshire and Worcestershire, where we have not yet recorded any buildings in detail, suggest that in these counties square kilns remained predominant. In Kent and Sussex few of the long rectangular kilns remain. The square kilns built later in the century rejoined the traditions embodied by the roundel in that they had firing by open grates and a similar shaped roof surmounted by a cowl but pyramidal rather than conical.

There is no doubt that this type of square kiln eventually replaced early roundels. An oasthouse in Lamberhurst, for example, which had two round kilns shown on the Tithe Map, underwent radical changes by 1869 when the survey for the first edition of the Ordnance Survey 1:2500 maps was made: the roundels were removed and the cooling floor was extended to almost twice its original size after which a square kiln was built at either end.

The reason for the return to square kilns is often said to be because the difficulties with uneven drying - 'cold corners' - had been encountered in round kilns as well. It may be that experiments with forced draught powered by steam engines which were carried out later in the century also helped this return since many such difficulties would thereby have been obviated. Another reason was offered by the anonymous author of an article on Sussex Hop Gardens published in 1882:

'The oast-houses, with their graceful cowls, are familiar objects to all residents or travellers in hop countries. They are not all externally alike, and internally their construction varies materially. Some are square, others round; the latter are the prettier to the eye, and in the opinion of many the more useful. But supposing their present occupation to be gone, they are not as easily adapted to other uses. The square shape is purposely adopted with a view to possible conversion into labourers' cottages'.[38]

The words were prophetic. They were born, no doubt, of the difficulties created by the depression in the general agricultural market which for the second time that century was beginning to face farmers, and by problems of crop failure which faced hop growers in that particular year. Another hundred years were to pass, however, before the prophecy of conversion was fulfilled, and then the people coming to live in the buildings were hardly to describe themselves as 'labourers' ! They were to occupy buildings which had become redundant because oasthouses still in use had reached a peak of efficiency such as no sixteenth-century hop drier could ever have imagined.

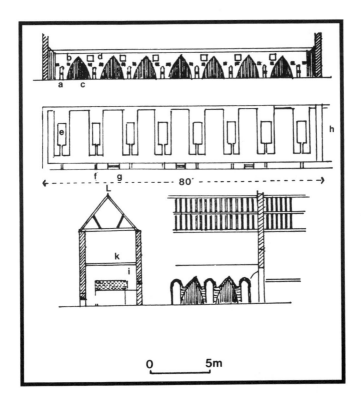

Fig. 28 The Development of the Square Kiln. An oasthouse in Morton's *Cyclopaedia of Agriculture* 1855. The similarities between this and the Surrey kiln, discussed by Loudon, are obvious, but in this case the juxtaposition of separate kilns is transformed into the provision of one long kiln. Beneath the drying floor any number of honeycombed furnaces could be provided. Draught entered the kilns under the pavement and also through square openings in the wall. Doors were also provided rather inconveniently high in the wall, so that the area round the furnaces could be cleared. Between the furnaces, arches opened into fuel stores and they were an innovation. As envisaged here the cooling floor adjoined one end of the kiln, which would have made loading and unloading a lengthy process.

Key:

a   Fire Holes
b   Holes to admit Cold Air to the Furnace
c   Arched Charcoal Storage Areas
d   Doors for the cleaning out of the Oasts
e   Horse (furnace) for equal dispersion of heat
f   Draught Holes
g   Windows
h   Stowage
i   Longitudinal Section of Horse
k   Haircloth Floor
L   Open Ridge Tiles to allow venting

45

CHAPTER 6
Late Nineteenth- and Twentieth-Century Development

'You are dealing with what was one of the most flourishing, and is one of the most important industries of the country, and an industry which we can singularly little afford to lose, because so many of our agricultural interests are passing through this period of depression'.   Lord Salisbury, 1887

Lord Salisbury, addressing the Commissioners who were to enquire into the reasons for the decline in the Hop Trade, was already looking back on fifteen to seventeen years of difficulty in the corn markets.[39] Serious loss of revenue here had affected other branches of agriculture. Shortage of money for the purchase of seeds and manure resulted in arable land reverting to grass as farmers in corn-growing areas desperately turned to dairy and beef cattle and to poultry rearing in order to try and keep going. To some extent, the hop growers had been able to hold out for rather longer because they were less dependent on corn; serious decline was deferred until the end of the 1880s.

The larger growers had for many years run the dual economy of hops and stock, feeding their hops with the manure produced and buying in less artificial manure than they would otherwise have needed. Both for them and for the smaller growers any increase in stock farming in the years of depression meant more home-produced and less bought manure for their hops - 'diversification' was also an economy. They were not to escape for ever. Eventually the major causes of the depression, namely free trade, cold storage and faster transportation were to affect their trade as well. As with the corn duty, the removal of the excise duty on hops in 1862 had resulted in a steady rise in imports. By the end of the century imports had been swelled both by a staggering rise in output of cheap hops in America and by a growing preference for lighter beers like those brewed in Germany.[40] For the lighter beers many of the English hops were unsuitable. For ordinary stock beers American hops were quite as suitable and much cheaper and brewers regularly used one third American hops to two thirds English. Fewer English hops were therefore needed.

New expertise in cold storage further affected the former structure of the market by making possible the long-term storage of hops. This enabled the large brewers to lay in huge stocks at very low prices in years of glut, and to keep out of the market altogether in years of scarcity. Any brewers who did need to buy could make up any shortage by turning to cheap, refrigerated imports brought across the oceans in the new improved steamships. This new ability to transport and store hops in peak condition deprived the growers in England of the customary rise in prices in years when the hop crop was short. To have hops for sale when other people's crops had failed had up till then been the foundation of all fortunes made from hops !

The new trend towards greater importation aggravated the problem which over the nineteenth century had become the most serious for the hop growers, that of over-supply. The days were gone when farmers needed to be urged to plant up with hops. Therefore a series of bad seasons in the 1890s only made an already bad situation worse. The worst hit were the small producers and the grubbing of hop gardens began. By 1908 it was claimed that 16,188 ha. (40,000 acres) had gone. In October that year a major demonstration in London on the part of hop growers and hop pickers demanded that the Government should re-impose the excise duty (Fig. 29).

The Government, with more pressing problems to attend to, turned a deaf ear to their demands. Hop growers were further upset in 1914 when the beer duty was raised, which resulted in a decrease in the amount of beer brewed. Again they petitioned for a duty on imported hops as the market was again found to be over-supplied. In 1916 imports were prohibited but the Government also decided to restrict the amount of beer brewed, and following new regulations beer was brewed at half the pre-War level. Further restrictions to one quarter of the pre-War level followed in 1917 and emergency measures were drawn up to allow the Government to handle the sale of the 1917 crop. The Hop Control was set up and did not finally lapse until 1925. During those years the growers sold their hops to the Hop Controller and received from him a pre-determined sum (decided annually), which allowed them a small profit. When there was a shortage, fixed amounts of foreign hops were imported. The scheme did not operate without difficulty and it provoked a lot of criticism from growers.[41]

Fig. 29 'Hop Saturday' October 1908. Farmers and pickers rode and marched through London, from Trafalgar Square to Southwark Hop Market, to demand the re-introduction of of the excise duty on imported hops. The Government did not heed their request.

47

The Control was eventually replaced by another body, English Hop Growers Limited. This was to rely on the voluntary co-operation of the growers and it eventually failed because not all the growers would agree to market their hops through its organisation. The prospect of chaos in an over-supplied market loomed again, the more so because the amount of beer being brewed was falling again by Government decree. Control over the market was re-imposed with the setting up of the Hops Marketing Board in 1932. The Board imposed quotas on registered growers and guaranteed a market for the hops grown within the quota. A period of calm returned to the hop world interrupted only by the arable demands of the Second World War.

One might have imagined that all technical progress would have ceased, given the difficulties at the beginning of the century, but today's technological advance is always dependent on yesterday's experiments, and ideas already under trial at the end of the nineteenth century came to fruition, even if sometimes delayed, in the twentieth.

Much stress has been laid on the development of the kilns during the first three quarters of the nineteenth century, but such increases as were seen in kiln capacity would have been impossible without parallel increase in the capacity of the stowage. In Kent, but not, so far as is known, in Sussex, new oasthouses built on the larger hop farms were designed with a third storey. This was used for the reception and temporary storage of the green hops. The middle floor served for cooling and pressing and the ground floor for storage of the filled pockets. The earliest recorded to date was built in 1876 at Down Farm, Lamberhurst (Fig. 30). Such large stowages usually served four or more kilns. Where there were fewer kilns another solution was found to the problem of avoiding damage during the storage of green hops: a slatted platform was built along the outside wall level with the first floor adjacent to the loading door. These probably came into use at the same time as the three-storey stowages but the date of erection of the first one is not known (Fig. 31).

If driers were skilled, these additions to the stowage probably brought the art of drying hops to a potential level of perfection beyond which it would have been hard to progress without the input of a new technology. Experiments with the use of fans to increase the air speed through the kilns began by using the drive power of the stationary steam engine.[42] The use of steam engines, either owned or hired, is known for many parishes for threshing and grinding and other farm uses. It would seem that such pioneering experiments must have been carried out initially by only a few of the major growers. The success of such experiments would have been readily recognised: the ability to push air through the hops greatly reduced the drying time and allowed the hops to be loaded to greater depths. The achievement of the fans was to increase yet again the capacity of the kiln without necessitating extensive alteration of the buildings. Moreover the speed of operation of the fan could be controlled and altered as necessary, and greatest of all in importance for the hop driers, was the elimination of the old problem of uneven drying and 'cold corners'.

By the end of the nineteenth century the attention of an Irish manufacturing firm, Davidson & Co., of Belfast, had been drawn towards hop drying. They were well known for their tea-drying plants, marketed under the trade name 'Sirocco', and experiments began to use similar machines for hop drying (Fig. 32). Installation of these machines began on hop farms in the early years of the twentieth century, but, given the economic climate of the times, the

Fig 30   A Three-storey Stowage, with tall brick-coned kilns at Down Farm, Lamberhurst parish, Kent, dated 1876.

Fig. 31   The Greenstage. When acreages had reached their nineteenth-century maximum, it became necessary to provide a 'greenstage' - a slatted platform - on which hops waiting to be dried could be stored without their beginning to sweat. This is another Lamberhurst example and is dated 1872.

49

machines were probably only taken up fairly slowly. Those who were able to invest appear to have been well pleased and very successful with them - if one can judge by the testimonies quoted in later catalogues![43]

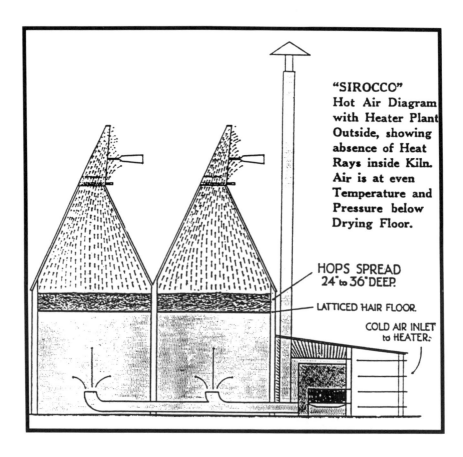

Fig. 32 Forced-draught Kilns. This illustration from an early twentieth-century catalogue put before the hop growers of the day a new concept: that of using a fan to blow the heat into the kiln. This was to be the final answer to the problem of contamination. It was taken up and improved upon and is still in use in kilns today.

'I would never go back to open fires for Hop Drying. With the 'Sirocco' Plant there is no fear of arsenic contamination. It is much more under control, and the hops can be dried at a lower temperature, rarely exceeding 130 Fah., which gives the hops a better 'rub', because more soft resins are retained. My regular load per an 8 to 10 hours drying is about 5 to 6 cwts. (254 - 305 kg.) of dried hops (500 bushels) on each kiln 20 feet (6.09m.) square. One 'Sirocco' Furnace to three kilns does this easily, which means 30 to 36 cwts. (1524 - 1830 kg.) of dried hops per day of 24 hours. More could be dried, but it does not pay to overload. The saving in fuel is considerable, as I use ordinary steam coal in place of Anthracite and also wood cut on the farm. Another advantage of the 'Sirocco' Plant is, the kiln and cooling flcor cost much less to build'.

That satisfied customer was a Mr. Rogers from Kent. His letter mentions nearly all the advantages which were to be obtained from these kilns. He failed only to say that the certainty of even drying meant that there was no longer any need to turn the hops as some driers did, loss of lupulin thereby being prevented, and that the hops cooled more readily after drying because the temperature inside the kiln could be instantly adjusted, eliminating the need to wait for the air to cool down.

The system clearly offered very great advantages and after 1919, when electricity became available in rural areas and when the hop market had settled down again after the disruptions of the First World War years, many growers invested in these kilns. From the savings they offered, some claimed to have regained the interest on the outlay, sometimes even the capital itself.

The furnaces could be fitted to existing buildings and many were. They brought about a reversal of one of the principles which had made kilns so tall towards the end of the nineteenth century. The regulation of the heat eliminated the need for extra air space beneath the kilns. Where cones were very tall, it often proved difficult to vent the mass of hot air pushed up by the fans quickly enough. Two solutions to these new problems were found: on existing kilns louvred vents were inserted in the cone above the drying floor and new kilns were reduced in height at the design stage. Some were built with walls half-brick thick or with walls of galvanised iron, it no longer being so important to insulate the lower storey of the kiln. The other great change brought about by this new style of drying was that cowls became redundant, as the hop drier was no longer dependent on natural draught. Louvred caps or long louvred ridges took their place (Fig. 33).

Bottom or 'pusher' fans forced the air up through the kiln. With the later electrification top or 'puller' fans were installed above the hops, usually just below the level of the cross beams which supported the pivot to the cowl. These fans were easier to install. They left the farmer free to choose whatever firing seemed best for his particular building and this was especially important when the second great innovation of the twentieth century was introduced.

Diesel, first used on farms in America at the end of the nineteenth century and extensively used in Great Britain by the 1930s, superseded all other types of furnace after the Second World War.[44] The design of the furnaces improved progressively; all were used in conjunction with fans which blew the heat into the kiln while keeping combustion products and contamination outside (Fig. 34). The introduction of both fans and diesel firing made the heating of the kiln much easier to control and brought great advances in the quality of the

Fig. 33A A Problem Solved, but Another Created. The ideas embodied in Fig. 32 produced problems in the very tall kilns of the late nineteenth century; the moisture-laden air could not be vented quickly enough. Many solved the problem by inserting vents or flaps just where the kiln roof first starts to gather in. Where new kilns were built, as here in Hawkhurst parish, Kent, they were not built so tall.

Fig. 33B A New-Style Kiln. Here the new 'forced-draught' technology has introduced a kiln built of galvanised iron. The problem of venting has been solved by the long louvred vent. This kiln was added to a mid-nineteenth-century oasthouse, in Iden parish, East Sussex.

Fig. 34 Early and Later Examples of Diesel Firing. The type of burner shown in the top photograph was introduced into many kilns and this necessitated the removal of the earlier firing apparatus. The burners shown in the lower photograph are fitted with sophisticated electronic controls, which ensure the correct temperature.

53

final product. With the stability offered to the industry by the quota system, further improvements were still being undertaken in the 1950s and 60s. Two-tier drying had become much easier to operate successfully once forced draught kilns had become accepted and many growers experimented with removable bins which made it possible to load and unload the kilns with minimum handling of the hops. Efforts were also made to recycle the hot air, ducting it back down into the plenum chamber* in order to reduce fuel costs.

Even those kilns are now outdated and in the most modern oasthouses the heat is regulated at various temperatures across a wide drying area. The hops are no longer unloaded into a kiln. Drying bins travel across the floor making carefully programmed stops at the different 'heat stations'. Sensors control switches to cut out or cut in the heat, guaranteeing a perfectly maintained temperature (Fig. 35). Gone are the head drier's idiosyncratic judgements based on smell, touch and 'experience'! Electrification also brought changes to the pressing system. Some presses were converted to electricity so that the hard work was taken out of the operation. Later a hydraulic baler press was perfected and both these and hydraulically operated, pocket presses are now found in the surviving oasthouses.

How long any oasthouses will survive is a matter for speculation. Latest developments in hop processing suggest that all buildings will soon become redundant, and as a new technique of dissolving hops in vast baths of liquid carbon dioxide is adopted the resulting product will be easily transported and preserved over years as are the hop pellets already in production.[45] The national crop itself is nothing like as large as it once was. The years of comparative prosperity and technological progress under the quota system were brought to an end through a combination of various factors. The ebb and flow of the market, already drastically altered by refrigeration and importation, was further affected by the perfecting of processes for producing hop 'essences'.

Verticillium Wilt, first recognised as a serious threat in 1924, has spread into every hop-growing area since.[46] Many gardens were devastated and many growers persuaded to give up hop growing. Eventually the problems caused were largely solved by the introduction of new wilt-resistant strains of hops bred by Wye College.

Then the entry into the European Economic Community brought the end of the Hops Marketing Board and with it went the guaranteed sale of quota hops. Rules were also introduced banning the growth of seeded hops, precisely those which grew best in Wealden soils! Only the better hop soils in Kent, Herefordshire and Worcestershire are able to produce the finer unseeded varieties successfully and economically. Even in those areas the fungal hop disease, Verticillium Wilt, has gradually taken a hold in the soils and has devastated the gardens. To make matters worse, recent prices have hardly covered the costs of production. Everything seems now to conspire towards a lasting contraction in the industry.

The buildings on which so much capital was expended, in which such pride was taken, are left redundant and deserve urgent attention. Many of them are the only surviving evidence of the once confident expectation of profit that many growers felt, an expectation which in written evidence is much harder to discern than is the heartfelt disapproval of the crop voiced by many of the commentators and agricultural improvers.

Fig. 35 The Scale and Technology of the Twentieth-century Industry. In the upper photograph, the hops are dried in bins which travel across the drying floor. After drying the hops are cooled, pressed and stored on a vast floor, seen in the lower picture. Lamberhurst parish, Kent.

CHAPTER 7
The Archaeology of the Oasthouse

The Hop Industry is a gamble, 'has therefore come to be an axiom. Yet with all its uncertainties this saying is not exactly true. Men who most perfectly understand the crop and most prudently allow for its uncertainties, have kept right along raising hops year after year, aiming at marketing about an even quantity of nice goods each season, and have found the industry rather more profitable in the end than any other crop grown in their neighbourhood'.

Myrick, 1899.[47]

Such has been the condemnation of the speculations of the hop grower that it is a wonder that anybody at all continued with the crop. That they did was frequently attributed to the fact that the capital invested in buildings and hop garden equipment was too great to be wasted. This was certainly true and must have played a part in many decisions to continue.

The evidence of the buildings, however, is more in accord with Myrick's statement quoted above. Nearly all bear the marks of renovation, many show that they had been repeatedly improved. That must imply the expectation of a comfortable financial return on the part of successive landowners, not in one or just a few isolated years, but over a period of time in which the good seasons were averaged out against the bad. John Noakes, responsible for some of the redevelopment of Forstal Farm oast in Lamberhurst, (Fig. 36), was able to say to a Parliamentary commissioner who asked:

'Did you make a considerable sum of money by it ?'

'Yes, I did well by growing hops'.[48]

He was certainly not alone in this. The secret of success lay in having the proverbial second string to the farming bow. For many large hop growers like John Noakes, the other mainstay was cattle. The two economies dovetailed: part at least of the manure from the large numbers of stock went onto the hops, the cattle themselves went into the expanding meat markets of London and the rotations followed for good fodder crops admirably suited the local soils which needed mixed husbandry to keep them in good heart.

When the buildings are studied in detail it is not uncommon to find that they have had two, three or four periods of development. Where sufficient remains of the original structure, a page of the history of the industry can be read from the fabric of the building. The detail of that page springs into sharper focus when documentary sources pinpoint both the periods at which the changes were made and the different people responsible for them. Before conversion, therefore, each building is potentially worthy of an archaeological and historical study, as the following examples will show.

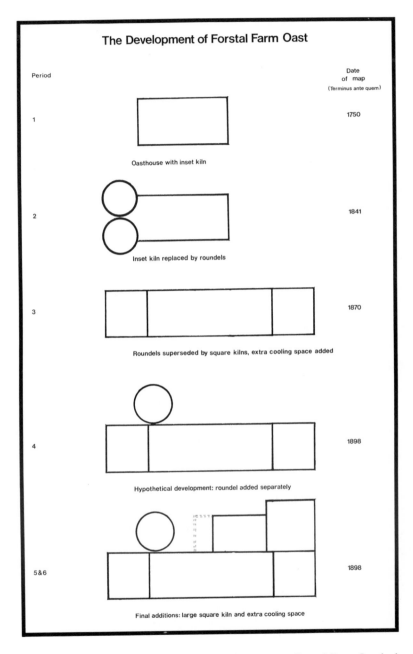

The Development of Forstal Farm Oast

Period

Date
of map
(Terminus ante quem)

1

1750

Oasthouse with inset kiln

2

1841

Inset kiln replaced by roundels

3

1870

Roundels superseded by square kilns, extra cooling space added

4

1898

Hypothetical development: roundel added separately

5&6

1898

Final additions: large square kiln and extra cooling space

Fig. 36 Nineteenth-century Enlargement of the Oasthouse at Forstal Farm, Lamberhurst parish, Kent. The diagram is based on changes visible in the fabric of the building and corroborated by map evidence.

57

Fig, 37A   An Old Oasthouse in Northiam parish, East Sussex, before conversion. The four roundels were the last of a series of refurbishments to the oasthouse.

Fig. 37B   The Roof Framing of the original eighteenth-century oasthouse was never removed when the later additions were made!

58

The oast recorded at Gate Court Farm, Northiam, stood typically close to a large pond and had four circular kilns built to the east of the stowage (Fig. 37A). Seen from the lane leading up to the farmstead, nothing was visible of its history; at the rear of the building, the lintel above the double doors at the north-western corner of the stowage bore the name C. Winser, and the date April 23rd., 1811, which could easily have been assumed to show the origin of the oasthouse. Inside, it was clear that its history had been much more complicated. The roof to the stowage had been constructed over the timbers of an earlier roof and close inspection revealed that quite a lot of an original four-bay oasthouse was still standing, wholly enclosed by a later building (Fig. 37B). A late seventeenth- or early eighteenth-century date is posited for that first building on the evidence of the timbers and of the layout of the building. In the two central bays it had two kilns, or perhaps one large one. The northern bay must have received the green hops, the southern must have served for cooling and pressing.

On the ground floor the jowls of two principal posts in the eastern wall of this building were turned out of normal alignment, suggesting that the building had at one time been extended on this side (see Fig. 38). It seemed reasonable to posit that one large or two smaller square kilns had been built alongside the original oasthouse here and examination of the Tithe Map showed that the building had indeed been 'L'-shaped at the time of that survey.[49] That map also showed that by then the original building had also been extended to the west, and it is likely that the two extensions were made as part and parcel of the same operation to increase the capacity of the oasthouse. Given the history of the industry as outlined in the preceding chapters, a late eighteenth- or early nineteenth-century date is a reasonable supposition. It tallies neatly with the date on the lintel but it has to be said that this could be explained in quite another way: that part of the building is in fact an ordinary hay barn which originally stood on Barham Farm and which was taken down and re-erected alongside the old oast some time after the two farms amalgamated into one, (the date of this amalgamation is not yet known). 1811 might therefore be the date at which the barn was originally erected on Barham farm.

It was certainly not originally erected in its present position: examination of the floor showed that it had been inserted into a barn which had not originally been floored and re-erection was the only explanation for the pieces of timber which had been added to the collars in order to lengthen them to make them fit a new roof construction. So when, finally, had the circular kilns been added, replacing the earlier rectangular extension (Fig. 38)? This last re-development was known to have taken place between 1860, when a sale map shows the rectangular extension still in position, and 1872 when the first edition of the Ordnance Survey 25-inch map shows the roundels in position.[50] Recent preliminary research into a set of valuations housed in Tenterden Museum unexpectedly revealed the date because during the 1860s annual valuations of the farm were made.[51] The addition of the roundels can be quite firmly dated to 1864, the period when the Hop Industry was at the height of its prosperity and shortly after the farm had passed into new ownership.

The roundels remained in use until the 1950s when the whole building was superseded by the construction of a new modern oast. That long last period was documented by succeeding generations of hop driers: starting in 1870, the dates of beginning and end of most of the seasons were stencilled on to the face

59

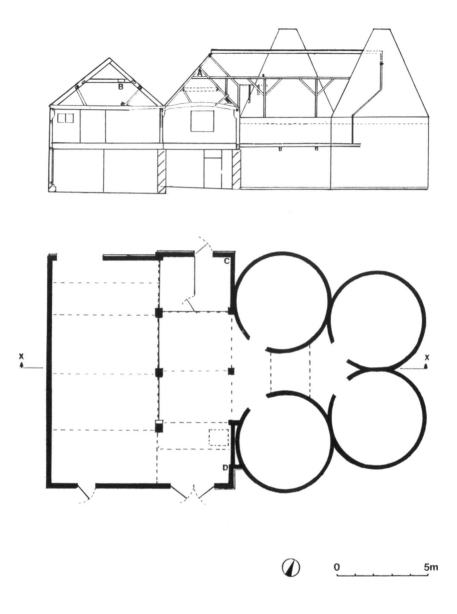

0   5m

Fig. 38 Ground-floor Plan and Section of this Northiam oasthouse (as shown in Fig. 37) show clearly the early building, in the middle, with its roof *in situ* (A) and the re-erected barn to the left of it, the joining-piece in the collar clearly visible at (B). The roundels replace earlier square kilns, whose former presence is indicated by the position of the principal posts at (C) and (D).

60

of the joists to the first floor. A comment, added for 1919, makes sense once the role of the Government of the day is understood. It read: 'bugering [sic] about' ! The dates do not start again until after the demise of the Hop Control !

The modern oast was brick-built. It was served by a hop-picking machine, housed close by, and had three kilns inset within the building. With the re-introduction of inset kilns the design of hop buildings had almost come full circle. Here, however, a diesel burner blew the hot air through the kilns and a long vent along the roof allowed it to escape once it had passed through the hops. The press was hydraulically operated and pressed the hops into bales, not pockets. More traditionally, the bales still had to be stencilled by hand and a few dates were also stencilled into the modern oast, continuing the practice begun in the old oasthouse. Now, as this book is written, the old oasthouse has been converted, the modern one, less picturesque and already outdated by new technology, has been demolished and yet another new building provided. When in use for hop drying, newly designed plenum chambers and bins are brought out on to the floor of the building. At the end of the hop season, they can be put away and the building is immediately ready to be put to some other use.

On farms where capital was more restricted, renovations to the buildings were less repeatedly carried out, and were usually effected with greater economy. They too remain as precious evidence of the ideas and conditions prevailing upon farmers at a given time. At Church Farm, Guestling, an oast on an altogether smaller scale was built in a parish where hop growing was less important than in Northiam. A new square kiln was added to an existing building at some time prior to 1833 when the 'drying part' was described as 'nearly new'.[52] The building to which this extension was added, a small three-bay, timber-framed structure, very similar in size to the oasthouses described on the Ticehurst Estate in the mid-seventeenth century, was quite possibly the original oasthouse on this farm, although conclusive documentary evidence to prove this does not appear to survive.

The interest here is twofold: even where hops were less extensively cultivated, they were sufficiently important to warrant capital outlay on buildings; this extension continued the tradition of the square or rectangular kiln precisely at the time when the new roundels were coming in. An added interest is that the kiln capacity was later increased again as the straight joints in the walls prove. If the older building was indeed the original oasthouse, then its capacity was more than doubled (Fig. 39). This kiln is quite unlike any other of similar period so far discovered. Was it efficient ? The answer to this question will probably never be known. There appears to have been a device for allowing the drier to travel above the drying hops on a movable plank. This idea was not widely adopted, as far as we know, until the beginning of the twentieth century. So was it original here ? There is no evidence to suggest that it was not. At present this oasthouse remains unconverted and some of the queries about the older half will be answered by careful excavation of the floor.

These examples could hardly be more different. Indeed, every building entered so far has had some different truth to reveal, some 'favourite plan', as Viscount Torrington justly observed. He went on to wonder why some uniform design had not been evolved:

' . . . . surely the landlords neglect their own interests in not having some fixed rules, in reference both to the oast house and the stowage, which would prevent

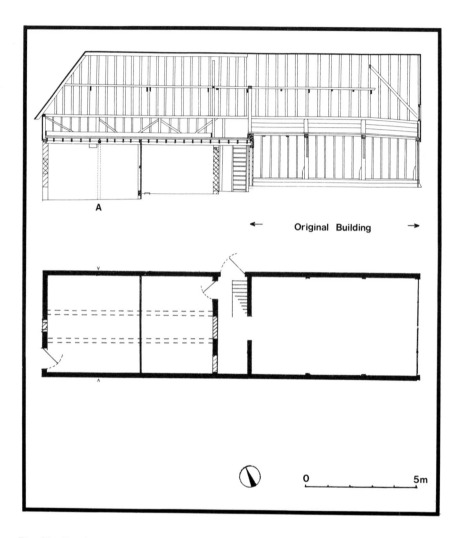

A

← Original Building →

0 _____ 5m

Fig. 39 Development and Change. The plan and section of this oasthouse in Guestling parish, East Sussex show three periods of building. The three bays to the right represent the first period - late seventeenth or early eighteenth century. To this was added a kiln which originally terminated at (A) and this was later extended to its present size. In a survey of 1833 this was referred to as 'the drying part, nearly new'.

the necessity of laying out such large sums on these buildings as has hitherto been the case. . . '.[53]
In so saying he failed to take into account the inevitable differences between individual levels of income, between the sizes and situations of the farms, and between the various economic climates - depression or prosperity - which governed the lives of the oast builders and users. Except in its primary function each oasthouse has to be different, and new details encountered still offer new information about principles of construction or the state of the industry.

Fig. 40 Traditional Hop-Picking. This photograph was taken in 1880, perhaps towards the end of that year's hopping - the fields behind look to have been stripped of their poles and bines. Every generation of each family could well be represented here. The pole-pullers and the measurer have joined the group and the two men on the left in the back row might have been the farmer and his son. (*This photograph is reproduced here by kind permission of Mr. P. Gillies.*)

Fig. 41 Hop-Pickers' Huts still standing just to the side of a small country lane in Lamberhurst parish, Kent. Note the wallpaper on the wall of the third hut. Even the front door is still there. Partitioned perhaps by curtains over a clothes line, each hut probably sheltered several members of the same family. Used with two cookhouses which stood opposite, for three or four weeks each year these huts were 'home'.

Fig. 42 The Oasthouse Party at Court Lodge, Bodiam marked the end of the hop-picking and the cooling floor was decorated for the occasion. There was singing and dancing, plenty to eat and drink and firm looking forward to next year's hopping on the same farm and with the same company. (*This photograph is reproduced here by kind permission of* The Hastings & St. Leonards Observer.)

POSTSCRIPT

Any new information that can still be gathered from standing buildings needs to be recorded *now* so that it can be put alongside what is already known about the hop industry.

The only well-known aspect is that of the hop-picking, the 'hop holiday' that scores of people, young and old, enjoyed (Fig. 40), in spite of the crowded and often insanitary conditions in which they lived (Fig. 41). These buildings are also part of the industry's history and record needs to be made of those that still remain. Too many have gone, leaving just their outline on a map.

Government legislation gradually dealt with the scandals of epidemic and overcrowding until a measure of comfort could be offered to most of the pickers. (That they returned year after year is testimony to the poverty and over-crowding that many endured for the rest of the year, with which successive governments took just as long to deal!) Despite so many accounts of dispute and brawling, fresh air and camaraderie were what they enjoyed and their enjoyment was brought to a fitting climax on more paternalistic farms at oast parties which celebrated the end of the hopping (Fig. 42).

As we see, such occasions survived into the 1950s but changes in terms of employment eventually made such numbers of people difficult to find. Mechanisation was therefore the answer. The degree of sophistication in the mechanisation now being applied to all aspects of the picking and drying ensure that such parties as are still thrown are much less populous affairs, enjoyed, in the main, by a handful of students.

Indeed, the new ideas being put into practice in Gate Court oasthouse and others being tried elsewhere effectively put an end to the need for specialised, purpose-built oasthouses. A large multi-purpose building with sufficient width of covered area is all that is required to allow the setting up of demountable plenum chambers at the beginning of the hop harvest. When it ends they can be packed away again!

It is therefore extremely unlikely that any of the old buildings will eventually be kept in use except in or as museums. Each disused building, therefore, needs to be at least examined, sometimes recorded in detail. It is no longer an 'endless task'. Many have already been converted and the pace of change will quicken again when the end of the present recession has been reached. The stripping down of the buildings and the stripping out of defective timbers can rob us of important clues and details (Fig. 43). Demolition (Fig. 44) robs us of everything if no record has been made! The point at which no original buildings will remain can now be envisaged. It has not yet been reached, but we do need a coherent planning policy from *all* Local Authorities which will provide for systematic examination before permission for conversion or demolition is granted.

Fig. 43A   The Conversion is well under way and there is much to be gained from keeping a careful watch on its progress. The relationship between the different periods of building may be further elucidated, hitherto hidden alterations may come to light and most if not all of the timberwork will be visible at the same time. Boreham Street, East Sussex.

Fig. 43B   The Excavation of a Kiln Floor often reveals the remains of the original firing preserved beneath a later floor. Here at an oasthouse in Guestling parish, East Sussex, the outline of the fireboxes either side of a central firing tunnel is beginning to be revealed. Where excavation is possible, it allows a more accurate record to be made.

66

REFERENCES

Foreword

1) Viscount Torrington, *On Farm Buildings with a few Observations on the state of Agriculture in the County of Kent*, (1845), p. 4.

Introduction

2) P. Clark, *The English Alehouse, a Social History 1200-1830*, Longman, London, (1983), pp. 31 & 32.

Chapter 1

3) H. Myrick, *The Hop, its Culture and Cure, Marketing and Manufacture*, Orange Judd Company, New York, (1899), p. 209.
4) A. Cronk, 'Oasts in Kent and East Sussex', *Archaeologia Cantiana*, 94, (1978), p. 107.
   D. & B. Martin, *Historic Buildings in Eastern Sussex*, Vol. 3. No. 6, Rape of Hastings Architectural Survey, Robertsbridge, (1982), p. 145.

Chapter 2

5) D.W. Crossley,(ed), *Sidney Ironworks Accounts, 1541-1573*, Camden Fourth Series, vol. 15, (1975), p. 54.
6) G. Mayhew, *Tudor Rye*, Centre for Continuing Education, Hove 1987, pp. 163, 239.
7) C. Brent, 'Rural Employment and Population in Sussex between 1550 and 1640', *Sussex Archaeological Collections*, (hereafter *S.A.C.*) vol. 114, 1976 p. 41.
8) R. Scot, *A Perfitte Platforme of a Hoppe Garden*, (1574, reprinted 1576, 1578, 1646).

Chapter 3

9) East Sussex Record Office (hereafter E.S.R.O.) PAR 377/6/1/1
10) D. & B. Martin, *op. cit.*, p. 136.
11) E.S,R.O. PAR 377/6/1/1.
12) E.S.R.O. DUNN MSS. 42/8.
13) E.S.R.O. DUNN MSS. 37/8.
14) Oxford English Dictionary.
15) E.S.R.O. DUNN MSS. 37/8.

Chapter 4

16) R. Bradley, *The Riches of a Hop Garden*, (1729), p. 4.
17) Quoted in P. Mathias, *The Brewing Industry in England, 1700-1830*, C.U.P., Cambridge, (1959), p. 482.
18) Quoted in P. Mathias, *ibid.*, p. 481.
19) R. Bradley, *op. cit.*, p. 5.
20) At the time of survey, considerable alteration had been made to the roof of this kiln. Nail holes on the surviving rafters suggested that internal framing had terminated in a central chimney at the ridge. It would have been broadly similar to that photographed at the Mayfield oasthouse discussed on page 26.

21) E.S.R.O. TD/E 133. The estimate of moderate acreages is based on the evidence of the Tithe Map.
22) *Instructions for Planting and Managing Hops, and for Raising Hop-Poles*, drawn up and published by the Dublin Society, Dublin, (1733), p. 10.
23) E.J. Lance, *The Hop Farmer*, (1838), p. 144.
24) R. Walton, *Oasts in Kent*, Christine Swift Bookshop, Maidstone, (1984), p. 109.

Chapter 5

25) E.S.R.O. W/INV 1448, ASH 1698.
26) E.S.R.O. ASH 1173.
27) A kiln lined with tin was suggested in John Worlidge's *Systema Agricultura*, published in 1669 (p. 135) in order to prevent contamination from the fuel and to avoid loss caused by turning the hops. Whether it was ever tried is not known. However, mention is made of an iron furnace already in use on some farms in Samuel Trowell's *New Treatise of Husbandry, Gardening and Other Curious Matters relating to Country Affairs*, published in 1739.
28) E.J. Lance, *op. cit.*, p. 144.
29) J.C. Loudon, *Encyclopaedia of Cottage, Farm and Villa Architecture*, (1833), p. 595.
30) 16th. Report of the Commissioners of Excise Enquiry, Hops, (1835).
31) Hastings Museum: Daws Diaries, 950.39. Both Thomas and his son Thomas Chester Daws kept diaries.
32) Messrs. Selmes and Langford were themselves hop growers with large acreages in the nearby East Sussex parishes of Beckley, Icklesham, Udimore & Rye.
33) E.J. Lance, *op. cit.*, p. 148.
34) G. Jones *et al.*, 'Oasthouses in Ewhurst Parish: Evidence for the History of an Industry', *S.A.C.* 126, (1988), pp. 195-224.
35) E.S.R.O. BAT 4572.
36) Loudon, *op. cit.*, p. 592.
37) J.C. Morton, *Cyclopaedia of Agriculture*, (1855), vol. 2, p. 63.
38) Anon. *Sussex Hop Gardens*, article reprinted with others in *Sussex Industries*, a small volume published by the *Sussex Weekly Advertiser*, Lewes (1888), pp. 84-104.

Chapter 6

39) Parliamentary Papers, 1890, XIII p. 275, *Enquiry into Causes of Steady Decrease of Acreage of Land Under Hop Cultivation and Serious Displacement of Labour Occasioned Thereby.*
40) H. Myrick, *op. cit.*, p. 12.
41) H.H. Parker, *The Hop Industry*, London, 1934.
42) R. Walton, *op. cit.*, p. 84.
43) Catalogue No. 32, Davidson & Co., Ltd., 'Sirocco' Engineering Works, Belfast.
44) J. Weller, *History of the Farmstead*, Faber, London, (1982), pp. 161-169.
45) J. Foster, 'Hop Growers Take Up Lager Challenge', *Sussex Express* 11/3/88.
46) H. Wormald, *Diseases of Fruits and Hops*, Crosby, Lockwood & Son, London, (1939).
47) H. Myrick, *op. cit.*, p.19.
48) Parliamentary Papers 1890, XIII, para. 1144.
49) E.S.R.O. TD/E/96.
50) Ordnance Survey: 1st. Edition 25-in. Sheet 31/7 (Sussex).
51) Valuations: Butler, Hatch & Waterman, Auctioneers, Tenterden, Tenterden Museum, Kent.
52) Ashburnham MSS: C 31, Hastings Museum. - now transferred to E.S.R.O.
53) Viscount Torrington, *op. cit.*, p. 4.

GLOSSARY

Bags: Larger than pockets, they held 127kg. (2 cwt.) and were used for the coarser hops.

Butt purlin: A longitudinal roof timber which is tenoned into main rafters giving support to the common rafters between the main trusses.

Diamond mullioned windows: In timber-framed buildings the mullions were diamond shaped in section and where these have disappeared a diamond shaped mortice is left in the frame where each one was fitted. This makes it possible to identify the exact position of the windows.

Greenstage: A slatted platform which was built on to the outside of the stowage; the slats again were designed to prevent the hops from sweating during storage before being loaded into the kiln.

Hills: After the root cuttings had started to grow the earth was heaped up around them. There were usually two or more cuttings to the hill.

Kilderkin: An archaic liquid measure which was equivalent to 81.83 litres (18 gallons).

Plenum Chamber: The ground floor of the kiln where the fire or furnace was situated.

Pocket: A long sack into which approximately 76 kg. (168 lb. = 1 ½cwt.)were pressed.

Pokes: Loosely woven bags in which the green hops were transported from the hop garden to the oasthouse; the open weave was especially employed to prevent the hops from sweating.

Poor Rates: These were levied on landowners by the parish for the upkeep of the poor people of that parish.

Resin: The petals of the cones contain glands which produce a golden resin called lupulin which bitters and helps preserve the beer.

Scuppet: A large, long-handled soft scoop made by fixing canvas across a timber frame. The person seen pressing hops in Fig. 5 is holding one.

Sets: Root cuttings taken from the plant in spring and nurtured to form stock for new hop gardens.

Spark Plate: A metal plate suspended from the drying floor above the furnace which had the dual purpose of shielding the drying hops from sparks from the fire and of acting as a baffle to spread the heat across the whole width of the floor.

Tithe Rents: The 'Tithe' or tenth part of the produce was given to the church to help maintain the clergy. In time this was commuted to a rent which was calculated by taking the number of pounds paid as rent and by multiplying that number by a fixed sum in the pound per acre. Hops, being considered as more valuable than ordinary crops, carried an 'extraordinary' charge which was greater than the ordinary rate and which varied from parish to parish.

Fig. 44A   Before Demolition. This Oasthouse near Rye, East Sussex, was recorded in 1982. The large stowage in the middle incorporated part at least of an earlier building and had originally served four roundels. After a disastrous fire two were replaced by square kilns. The cowls on all four kilns were later replaced by louvred caps after the introduction of forced draught and diesel firing. (*This photograph is reproduced here by kind permission of Mr. A. Dickinson.*)

Fig. 44B   The End of the Demolition. The oasthouse pictured above had nearly gone, but not without trace - we have a good record of the building.

BIBLIOGRAPHY

Anon.   *Sussex Hop Gardens*, (1882), reprinted in *Sussex Industries*, (1888).

Baker, D.   *Agricultural Prices, Production and Marketing with particular reference to the Hop Industry of N.E. Kent, 1680-1760*, Ph.D. Thesis, University of Kent, 1976, published by G.P. Garland Publishing Inc., New York & London, (1985).

Bradley, R.   *The Riches of a Hop Garden*, (1729).

Brent, C.   'Rural Employment and Population in Sussex between 1550 and 1640', *Sussex Archaeological Collections* (hereafter *S.A.C.*), vol. 114, (1976).

Brown, J.F.   *Guinness and Hops*, Guinness & Co. publication, (1980).

Clark, P.   *The English Alehouse, a Social History, 1200-1830*, Longman, London, (1983).

Cronk, A.   'Oasts in Kent and East Sussex', *Archaeologia Cantiana*, vol. 94, (1978), pp. 99-110 & vol. 95, (1979), pp. 241-254.

Crossley, D.W. *Sidney Ironworks Accounts, 1541-1573*, Royal Historical Society, (Camden Fourth Series), University College, London, (1975).

Dublin Society. *Instructions for Planting and Managing Hops*, (1733).

Hall, A.D. &   *A Report on the Agriculture and Soils of Kent, Surrey and*
Russell, E.J.   *Sussex*, Board of Agriculture & Fisheries, London, (1911).

Jones, G. *et al.* 'Oasthouses in Ewhurst Parish: Evidence for the History of an Industry', *S.A.C.* vol. 126, (1988).

Lance, E.J.   *The Hop Farmer*, (1838).

Loudon, J.C.   *Encyclopaedia of Cottage, Farm and Villa Architecture*, (1833).

Marshall, W.   *The Rural Economy of the Southern Counties*, (1798).

Martin, D. & B. *Historic Buildings in Eastern Sussex*, vol. 3 no. 6, Rape of Hastings Architectural Survey, Robertsbridge, (1982).

Mathias, P.   *The Brewing Industry in England 1700-1830*, C. U. P., Cambridge, (1959).

Mayhew, G.   *Tudor Rye*, Centre for Continuing Education, University of Sussex, Hove, (1987).

Morton, J.C.   *Cyclopaedia of Agriculture*, (1855).

Myrick, H.   *The Hop, Its Culture and Cure, Marketing and Manufacture*, Orange Judd Co., New York, (1899).

Parker, H.H.   *The Hop Industry*, London, (1934).

Scot, R.   *A Perfitte Platform of a Hoppe Garden*, (1574, reprinted 1576, 1578, 1644).

Torrington, Lord.   *On Farm Buildings with a few Observations on the State of Agriculture in the County of Kent*, (1845).

Trowell, S.   *A New Treatise of Husbandry, Gardening and Other Curious Matters relating to Country Affairs*, (1739).

Walton, R.A.E.   *Oasts in Kent*, Christine Swift Bookshop, Maidstone, (1984).

Weller, J.   *History of the Farmstead*, Faber, London, (1982).

Wormald, H.   *Diseases of Fruits and Hops*, Crosby, Lockwood & Son, London, (1939).